CULTURE SMART!

BULGARIA

THE ESSENTIAL GUIDE TO
CUSTOMS & CULTURE

JULIANA TZVETKOVA

KUPERARD

"The real voyage of discovery consists not in seeking new landscapes, but in having new eyes."

Adapted from Marcel Proust, *Remembrance of Things Past.*

ISBN 978 1 78702 327 7

British Library Cataloguing in Publication Data
A CIP catalogue entry for this book is available
from the British Library

First published in Great Britain
by Kuperard, an imprint of Bravo Ltd
59 Hutton Grove, London N12 8DS
Tel: +44 (0) 20 8446 2440
www.culturesmart.co.uk
Inquiries: publicity@kuperard.co.uk

Design Bobby Birchall
Printed in Turkey

The Culture Smart! series is continuing to expand.
All Culture Smart! guides are available as e-books, and many
as audio books. For further information and latest titles visit
www.culturesmart.co.uk

ABOUT THE AUTHOR

JULIANA TZVETKOVA is an academic and intercultural intelligence trainer. Born and educated in Bulgaria, she has an M.A. from Sofia University's Faculty of Classic and Modern Philology. After graduation she did translating, interpreting, and research, and worked for Bulgarian National Television. In 1998 Juliana moved with her family to Canada where she joined the Communications Faculty of Centennial College. She worked for Centennial around the globe for more than twenty years, and began her intercultural training career in Dubai. Today she combines her intercultural and educational work with writing. She has contributed to encyclopedias and is an author of *Pop Culture in Europe* and *Culture Smart! Canada*.

CONTENTS

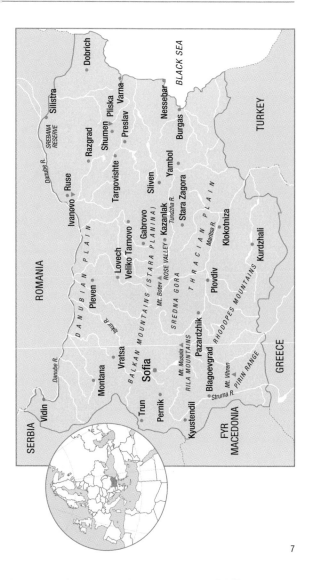

INTRODUCTION

One of the oldest countries in Europe, Bulgaria became the youngest member of the European Union on January 1, 2007. If there is a word that best describes the Bulgarians, it is "proud." Founded in 681 CE, the country takes pride in being the oldest European nation-state never to have changed its name. It is also proud to have given the world the Cyrillic alphabet, the first electronic wristwatch, the electronic digital computer, and some of the twentieth-century's greatest opera singers. Most of all, Bulgarians are proud of their long history and the natural beauty of their land: "Bulgaria" and "paradise" are often used in the same sentence.

Situated on the Balkan Peninsula, Bulgaria was at the crossroads of Europe and Asia and a melting pot of ancient cultures. Today, four pan-European transportation corridors connect Western Europe to Eastern and Southeastern Europe and Asia across its territory. Invasions and waves of migration, starting from neolithic and classical times, have contributed to its unique cultural mosaic. The seventh-century Bulgarian empire dominated the Balkans and was a powerhouse of Slavonic culture. Later, Ottoman conquest and Soviet influence left their mark on the national psyche.

Bulgaria's colorful traditions are rooted in an ancient pagan past and twelve centuries of Orthodox Christianity. The new year starts with the lucky backtapping *surovakane* rite. Bulgarians celebrate name days, such as the patron saint of winemaking, Trifon Zarezan; Baba Marta, marking the end of winter, when red and white yarn *marteniza* adornments are worn; the day of the Slavonic alphabet, of Bulgarian enlightenment and culture; and very many other holidays. To throw a great party one needs great company, and the Bulgarians are famous for their hospitality, warmth, well-stocked tables, and lively music. Easygoing, and with a great sense of humor, they enjoy making new friends and know how to cherish old ones.

Today, Bulgaria's seaside and winter resorts attract many visitors, while its rapidly developing economy draws investors from around the world. This book is for vacationers, adventure seekers, businesspeople, and lovers of ancient culture and art. It will familiarize you with this small but beautiful land and its complex people. It describes the formative influences on Bulgarian society, and the way Bulgarian people interact with foreigners and each other. It offers important insights and practical advice that will smooth your path and deepen your experience in this intriguing country.

Dobre doshli v Bulgaria, skapi priateli!
Welcome to Bulgaria, dear friends!

Official Name	Republic of Bulgaria	Adopted in 1991 after the first democratically held elections
Population	6,835,000	More than 1.5 million have emigrated or left to work abroad since 1989 when borders were opened following the fall of communism.
Capital City	Sofia, since 1879. Population roughly 1.5 million	Known as Sofia since 1376. Older names are Serdika (Roman), Triadiza (Byzantine), Sredetz (Bulgar).
Major Cities	Plovdiv, Varna, Burgas	
Area	42,855 sq. miles (110,994 sq. km)	
Borders	Romania, Serbia, Macedonia, Greece, Turkey	Black Sea, Danube River (mostly with Romania)
Climate	Continental climatic zone (north) Humid subtropical climate (east) Mediterranean (south)	Four seasons in continental temperate zone; the south and coastal regions have milder weather patterns.
Currency	Lev (BGN) One lev = 100 stotinki	The lev is pegged to the euro. One euro = lev (BGN) (лв) 1.955. Bulgaria expects to join the Eurozone in 2024.
Ethnic Makeup	Bulgarian 85%; Turkish 8.8%; Roma 4.9%; Macedonians, Tartars, and Armenians 0.4%	

Languages	Bulgarian (official), Turkish, Roma (minority)	Cyrillic is the official script.
Religion	Orthodox Christianity is the dominant religion. Others: Islam, Judaism, Catholicism, Protestantism	
Government	Parliamentary republic. The National Assembly (Narodno sabranie) has 240 members elected every four years.	The Council of Ministers holds executive power, and the President is elected by direct vote for a five-year term.
Media	State TV and private television networks. State: BNT (BNT1, BNT2, BNT World)	Private: bTV (6 channels); TV7 (2 channels); NOVA television; DIEMA (5 channels)
Print and Digital Press	Bulgarian News Agency; Bulgarian News Network (BNN); Frog News (culture, sports, tourism); Novinite.com (major news provider)	*Media Times Review* (online magazine); *Sofia Echo* (weekly paper); *Standart News* (online English edition)
Electricity	220 volts, 50 Hz	Standard European two-prong plugs; adaptors are needed for North American and UK appliances.
Telephone	Bulgaria's country code is +359.	Sofia code 02; Plovdiv code 04
Time Zone	Eastern European Time (EET) UTC/GMT + 2 hrs	Eastern European Summer Time (EEST) UTC/GMT + 3 hrs

CHAPTER ONE

LAND & PEOPLE

GEOGRAPHY

Situated in Southeastern Europe on the northeast part of the Balkan Peninsula, the Republic of Bulgaria covers 42,685 sq. miles (110,994 sq. km), and is Europe's sixteenth-largest country. Greece and Turkey are its southern neighbors; Serbia and the former Yugoslav Republics of Macedonia and Montenegro lie to the west; the Danube River separates it from Romania to the north; and the Black Sea coast delineates its eastern border. Despite its comparatively small size, Bulgaria has an amazing variety of landforms. More than 65 percent of its territory is covered by plains and plateaus, while a quarter of the rest is mountainous. There are four main regions from north to south.

Marking most of Bulgaria's northern border with Romania, the Danube flows through a vast plateau that extends south, reaching the Balkan range. The Danubian

Coastal wall in the city of Sozopolon on the Black Sea.

Plain lies between the Serbian border to the west and the northern Black Sea coast to the east. It rises gently from cliffs along the river to 3,117 feet (950 m) before reaching the mountain range. This plateau contains Bulgaria's most fertile soil, which produces most of its wheat, sunflowers, grapes, sugar beet, and tobacco.

The Balkan Mountains stretch from the Timok Valley in Serbia to the Sofia Basin in west-central Bulgaria, and thence eastward to the Black Sea. The range is about 370 miles (600 km) long and up to about 30 miles (50 km) wide. Mount Botev, the highest point, rises to 7,795 feet (2,376 m). The range then reaches and juts

Majestic rocks in Belogradtschik.

into the Black Sea as Cape Emine. Stara Planina (the Old Mountain), as the range is known in Bulgaria, is composed of granite and crystalline rock, but is much better known for the quality timber of its forests, which has led to the deforestation of large parts.

The Balkan Mountains divide Bulgaria into two almost equal drainage systems. The larger system drains northward to the Black Sea by way of the Danube. This system includes the entire Danubian Plain and a stretch of land running inland from the coastline. The second system drains the Thracian Plain and most of the higher lands of the south and southwest to the Aegean Sea.

Arda River in the Rhodopes Mountains.

Bulgaria has only one navigable river, the Danube, but many of its other rivers and streams are used for the production of hydroelectric power and irrigation.

To the south of the Balkan range are the Lowlands and Sredna Gora, a narrow ridge nearly a hundred miles (about 160 km) long and not very high. There lie more fertile valleys, the Valley of the Roses being the most famous among them for the production of rose oil. The southern slopes of the Balkan Mountains and the Sredna Gora merge into the Thracian Plain. Roughly triangular in shape, the plain begins east of the mountains near Sofia and widens eastward to the Black Sea. It includes

Rila Mountain scene.

the Maritsa River Valley and the lowlands that extend
from the river to the Black Sea. Like the Danubian Plain,
much of the Thracian Plain is uneven, yet most of its
terrain is arable, and is Bulgaria's fruit and vegetable
garden as well as its major winemaking region. To the
south the plain reaches the foothills of the Rhodopes,
a mountainous area famous for its unparalleled beauty
and its wealth of water resources and minerals such as
zinc and lead.

The Rhodopes is a system of ridges and deep river
valleys, forming the largest mountain massif in the
country, covering more than 9,000 sq. miles (14,500 sq. km),

83 percent of which are on Bulgarian territory, and the rest in Greece. The western Rhodopes consists of two mountains: Rila, south of Sofia, and Pirin, in the southwestern corner of the country. The Rila range includes Mount Musala (9,760 feet, or 2,975 m), the highest peak on the Balkan Peninsula. Rila also has a dozen other peaks rising over 8,530 feet (2,600 m), and is characterized by scant bare rocks and glacial lakes above the tree line. The lower peaks, however, are covered with alpine meadows that give the range an overall impression of green beauty. Rila boasts more than two hundred lakes and many mineral springs, with the Seven Lakes of Rila and the Rila National Park among the mountain's most popular tourist spots. The Pirin Mountains are characterized by rocky peaks and stony slopes. Its highest peak, Mount Vihren (9,563 feet, or 2,915 m) is the second highest in Bulgaria.

CLIMATE

Despite its small area, Bulgaria has a variable and complex climate. The country is located between two distinct climatic zones—continental and Mediterranean. The mountains and the valleys are either barriers or channels for the continental air masses, affecting the weather in patchwork patterns: swift changes within hours are not unusual. The larger part of the country is subjected to the continental climatic zone, as there is no obstacle between continental air masses and the lowland Danubian Plain. The cool continental air mass produces a lot of snow, while the Mediterranean influence intensifies during late summer and results in hot, dry weather. The barrier effect of the Balkan range is felt all over the country: on average, northern Bulgaria is about one degree cooler and receives about 7.6 inches (192 mm) more rain than the plains and valleys of southern Bulgaria. The Black Sea's influence on climate is limited to the immediate areas along the coast.

The Balkan Mountains stop the free circulation of continental air masses, while the Rhodope massif marks the northern limits of Mediterranean weather systems domination. The area in between—the Northern Thracian Plain—is influenced by a combination of the two systems, of which the continental predominates. This combination produces a plains climate with long summers and high humidity. Because it is a transitional area, average temperatures and precipitation are unpredictable and the climate in this region is generally more severe than that of other parts of Europe in the same latitude.

Average annual precipitation in Bulgaria is about 24.8 inches (630 mm). The plains in the north and south, the Black Sea coastal area, and a small part of the Northern Thracian Plain usually receive less than 20 inches (500 mm). The mountains have the most rainfall in the country, which may average more than 100 inches (2,540 mm) per year.

The capital, Sofia, is located in a valley basin with temperature inversions that bring poor air quality, especially in winter, but its elevation (about 1,739 feet, or 530 m) provides for moderate summer temperatures and tolerable humidity. Sofia is also sheltered from the northern European winds by the mountains that surround its trough-like basin. Temperatures in Sofia average 32°F (0°C) in January and about 71.6°F (22°C) in August. The city's rainfall is near the country average.

Winters are generally cold and snowy, and milder in the southern regions of the country; there are periods in which the temperature remains below the freezing point for weeks. The average winter temperature for the northern regions is about 33.8°F (1°C); in the south 39.2°F (−4°C). Snowstorms occur often, most notably and severely in the north. On January 2, 2008, in the town of Svishtov, 3.37 feet (103 cm) of snow cover fell in less than twenty hours. The recorded minimum temperature of −36.9°F (−38.3°C) occurred west of Sofia, near Trun.

The highest mountains—Rila and Pirin in the southwestern part of the country— are 3,281 feet (1,000 m) above sea level and have an alpine climate. The southernmost parts of the Struma and Maritsa river valleys enjoy a humid, subtropical climate with a lot of sunshine, as do the eastern Rhodopes. The extreme southwestern part of Bulgaria is the warmest. In summer, temperatures there often exceed 84°F (30°C).

The Black Sea coastal climate is milder, but strong

winds and violent local storms are not unusual in winter. Winters along the Danube River are bitterly cold, while the naturally protected low valleys along the Greek and Turkish borders may be as mild as the areas along the Mediterranean or Aegean coasts.

The Bulgarian sun is truly miraculous: what starts out as a chilly spring or fall morning with 32°F (0°C) can turn into a wonderfully warm, inspiring 71.6°F (22°C) afternoon. Similarly, temperatures can rise to 68°F (20°C) on a bright, sunny winter's day in the mountains. The best thing to do is dress in layers and be prepared for swiftly changing weather patterns.

REGIONS AND MAJOR CITIES

Western Bulgaria

To the southwest, Mount Musala is surrounded by the stunning glacial lakes of Rila in the highest mountain range in Bulgaria and the Balkans, and the sixth highest in Europe. In the massif nests the Rila monastery, one of the region's most significant cultural, architectural, and historic monuments, and a World Heritage Site since 1983.

Another World Heritage Site, the Pirin National Park, lies nearby. It's just one of twelve national reserves, home to unique flora and fauna and stunning scenery, and is a great place for trekking in summer and skiing in winter.

Sofia is situated on the route historically connecting Western Europe to the Byzantine East. Because of its strategic significance since Roman times, the city became a major commercial and military center and played an important role in the history of the Balkans. Today Sofia is home to more than a million and a half Bulgarians, who enjoy a rich and lively cultural life, offered by numerous theaters, opera houses, cinemas, and concert halls, and the national ballet and symphony orchestra. It's also the epicenter of Bulgarian political and business life.

Northern Bulgaria

The Danubian Plain covers most of northern Bulgaria and is the main breadbasket of the country. It also

The 100-meter-high Madara Horseman rock relief in Shumen, northeast Bulgaria.

holds 30 percent of its vineyards and is famous for its Cabernet Sauvignon. The grapes are still harvested by hand. It's rich in copper, manganite, lignite, and oil, and is home to two more World Heritage Sites— Srebarna, a nature reserve and lake on the Via Pontica bird migration route, and the churches of Ivanovo, a monolithic complex of churches, chapels, and monasteries hewn out of solid rock. Bulgaria's most cherished symbol, the Madara Horseman, an early medieval rock relief and another World Heritage Site, can be seen near the town of Shumen, in the northeast of the country.

Ruse is Bulgaria's main city on the Danube. It's an important cultural, commercial, and industrial

Historical architecture in Ruse city center.

center because of its strategic location on the longest waterway of the European Union. With a population of 180,000, it is the fifth-largest city in the country, known as "little Vienna" for its beautiful architecture.

Southern Bulgaria

The fertile Thracian Plain yields an abundance of fruit and vegetables, and its vineyards and wineries have been producing wine since the times of the Dionysian mysteries. To this day the descendants of the ancient Thracians love wine, music, and dancing to free them from their worries and fears. Stretching between the Rhodope range and Sredna Gora, with the Maritsa River meandering through it, Thrace is home to numerous tombs, such as the world-renowned Thracian tomb of Kazanlak, which has been a World Heritage Site since 1979.

Plovdiv, the fourth-oldest continually inhabited settlement in Europe, dates from 6000 BCE. The city's history is a fascinating journey in time, marked by its seven different names. The city of the seven hills enjoys a humid, subtropical climate, with a lot of sunshine in the summer months.

To the south of the Thracian Plain rises the intensely beautiful and richly historical Rhodopes Mountains. The ancient Thracian sites of Perperikon and Belintash—the medieval castles, churches, monasteries, and picturesque villages with traditional medieval architecture—mesmerize and enchant the visitor. The mountains have the largest coniferous woods on the Balkans and are rich in mineral springs and abundant water resources. The climate is mild and Mediterranean-influenced.

Eastern Bulgaria

The Bulgarian Black Sea coast is a major attraction not only for sun-starved visitors from the landlocked countries of Western Europe; its white and golden sandy beaches are more than 80 miles (130 km) long and make this the most appealing vacationing spot for Bulgarians in summer. Prior to 1989 it was known

The Cathedral of the Assumption in Varna, eastern Bulgaria.

as the Red Riviera; now it's the Bulgarian Riviera. History lovers will be fascinated by ancient towns like Nessebar—another World Heritage Site. The humid subtropical climate and long hot summers, from May until October, make the Black Sea coast the ideal place to take a relaxing break.

Varna, Bulgaria's third-largest city, is the largest city on the country's Black Sea coast. Dating from 4,500 BCE, the world's oldest hoard of gold treasure was discovered near the port of Varna in 1972. Today Varna is the main port for both naval and commercial shipping, and hosts numerous national and international cultural events.

THE PEOPLE

Bulgarians belong overwhelmingly to the Southeastern Slavic ethnic group. They descend from the inhabitants of the former Thracian provinces of the Roman and Byzantine Empires on one hand, and the early Slavs and the Proto-Bulgars on the other. With an estimated population of more than a million in 700 CE, the Bulgarian population had grown to 2.6 million six hundred years later, before surrendering to the Ottoman invaders from Asia Minor.

In the 1980s Bulgaria's population reached nearly 9 million, but the expulsion of Bulgarian Turks, the emigration of a million or more people after the collapse of the Communist regime, and a steadily decreasing birthrate have all contributed to the 2021 population count of 6,520,314. The CIA World Factbook places Bulgaria at 74 of 227 countries and territories in the category of Gross Domestic Product, and at 226 out of 231 in Population Growth, with a negative 0.67 percent population growth rate in 2022.

The rapidly decreasing population is a matter of grave concern. Fears that too many young Bulgarians leave to study abroad are substantiated by the fact that only Estonia beats Bulgaria in having the highest emigration rate in the European Union. In the aftermath of the drastic political changes in 1989, a lot of highly skilled and well-educated people left, thus creating a serious brain drain in the country. Another popular fear is that Bulgarians are doomed to disappear, based on some experts' opinions that by 2050 there will be fewer than 5 million left, turning the present-day Slavic Christian Orthodox majority into a minority, and Romani and Turkish minorities into majorities. This pessimism is deeply rooted in the highly skeptical Bulgarian mindset.

However, there is an optimistic streak, too. Young people leave the country, but many of them return, and emigration rates have slowed down in recent years. The global financial crisis of 2008 forced quite a few of its nationals to return to Bulgaria, with its lower cost of living. Besides, following the turbulent years that marked the end of the twentieth century, there was a

mini baby boom, with twice as many children born
in 2001–02 than in the economically and politically
unstable period between 1996–97. Government
policies to encourage childbirth are also in place: in
2009, a state fund was created to provide access to
in vitro fertilization and over 13,000 women have
benefited from this so far. Since Bulgaria joined the
European Union, West Europeans have contributed
to the revival of Bulgarian villages by buying cheap
properties in the country. They were attracted by the
beautiful natural surroundings and mild climate, and
they are here to stay.

According to the 2021 Census, Bulgaria's ethnic
and demographic fabric is as follows: 85 percent
Bulgarians, 8.8 percent Turks, 4.9 percent Roma, and
small numbers of Macedonians, Tatars, and Armenians
totaling 0.4 percent. The official language of the
country is Bulgarian; Turkish and Roma are spoken
by the main ethnic minorities.

Turks

According to Minority Rights Group International,
prior to the end of the Second World War, the Turks
in Bulgaria lived in cultural, political, and social
isolation—with their own schools and court systems—
leaving many unable to speak Bulgarian. Following
the Communist takeover, the regime embarked on a
program of integrating the Turks into the Bulgarian
mainstream, culminating in the closing of all religious

schools and the nationalization of private, community-run schools: Bulgarian became a compulsory subject, while Turkish was removed from schools by 1975 and from the media by 1984. In the late 1980s, in a bid to create a united Socialist state, the government forced the Turks to renounce their Muslim names and customs altogether and adopt Bulgarian names. These policies only further encouraged the Turkish minority to organize mass protests and hunger strikes, leading to a massive, largely voluntary emigration by ordinary Turks out of Bulgaria. Minority Rights Group International estimates the number of those who had left by August 1989 at 350,000—however, about one-third returned after the fall of the Communist regime. This exodus became known as "The Great Excursion."

Today, Bulgarian Turks enjoy political representation, practice Islam freely, and Turkish is included in the curriculum and in the media. Generally speaking, the Turkish minority continues to uphold its customs, traditions, and culture.

Roma

Largely ignored by the Communist regime, the Roma became an important issue the moment Bulgaria started preparing for European Union membership. The country had to prove its willingness to improve conditions for its minorities, ease ethnic tensions, and preempt political conflicts in the Balkans. Funded by the EU, the Bulgarian government adopted a project, called the Framework Program, for the integration of the Roma into Bulgarian society in April 1999. This program established the core principles and measures to fight discrimination and unemployment, to increase levels of education and health care, and provide for the cultural protection of the Roma minority. The results of this program have yet to be seen; many Bulgarians continue to hold unfavorable views of their Roma compatriots, and stereotypes persist.

A BRIEF HISTORY

The Bulgarian lands witnessed the emergence of organized social life as early as the middle Paleolithic period (100,000–40,000 BCE). By the third millennium BCE these lands had fallen under the influence of the Thracians—Indo-European tribes who were masters of metalworking, particularly in silver and gold, and known for their horsemanship. A Thracian king, Rhesus, took part in the war against Troy. Another famous Thracian king, Orpheus, became the hero of one of the most romantic and tragic love stories in ancient history.

The Thracians had a serious weakness, however. They were not in the least interested in cohesion and political organization. As a result, the powerful Macedonian state clashed with the Thracians and by 335 BCE had easily subordinated them. Subsequently

Thracian soldiers and cavalry took part in Alexander the Great's march to India. When the Romans descended on the Balkans in the third century BCE, they quickly subjugated the Thracian tribes and established order and an efficient rule, laying the foundations of prosperity and stability not seen in the region before. An intricate network of roads connected the Balkans east to west and north to south, and the region flourished due to increased traffic, trade, and commerce. When the Roman Empire split in two, Constantinople, the capital of Byzantium, became an important cultural and political center that played a crucial role in the history of Bulgaria for the next thousand years.

In the second century CE, the Proto-Bulgars came to Europe from their old homeland, the Kingdom of Balhara in the Mount Imeon area—today the Hindu Kush, in northern Afghanistan. There is a hypothesis that ethnically they were of mixed Asian and Indo-European origin, making them "cousins" of the Afghans and Iranians. An ancient manuscript claims that the first Proto-Bulgarian state in Europe was founded by Khan Avitohol in 165 BCE. In the fourth and fifth centuries CE Proto-Bulgarian tribes invaded parts of Central and Eastern Europe, settling in Pannonia (present-day Hungary), Albania, and Ukraine. Bulgarian gold treasure from this era has been found in Nagyzsentmiklos (Transylvania), Vrap (Albania), and Malaya Pereshchepina (Ukraine), the last of which is the burial treasure of Khan Kubrat, father to Khan Asparukh, the founder of the Bulgarian state. At the same time—in the fifth century CE—another large group of tribes, the Slavs, were making their way into the Balkans. Unlike some of the other invaders, such as the Alans, the Goths, and the Huns, who moved on after their failure to plunder Constantinople, they had come here to stay. Striking an alliance with the Proto-Bulgars, they started assaulting the Byzantines, and won a decisive victory over Emperor Constantine IV Pogonatus in 680.

The First Bulgarian Kingdom (681–1018)

In 681 CE the new Bulgar state was recognized by the Byzantine Empire. Its leader, Khan Asparukh, founded the capital, Pliska, and for the next century and a half the Bulgarians expanded their rule to the southwest and the northwest, won some notable victories over Byzantium, and introduced a proper legal system. In 864 King Boris I of Bulgaria adopted Orthodox Christianity, and his son, Simeon I (893–927), ushered in Bulgaria's Golden Age. Art and literature flourished. The Bulgarian monks Naum and Kliment—disciples of the Byzantine missionaries Cyril and Methodius—introduced the Cyrillic alphabet into Bulgaria in the early tenth century. This enabled the Bulgarian Church to use Slavo-Bulgarian as the language of the liturgy and preserved it from total Greek domination. Naum, Kliment, and their disciples initiated the translation of ecclesiastical literature into Bulgarian, as well as the creation of original secular literature. The cities of Preslav and Ohrid became renowned centers of education and culture, which soon spread to Serbia, Bosnia, Croatia, Transylvania, Wallachia, Moldavia, and Kievan Rus.

The end of the tenth century saw a rapid decline to a tragic end. Legend has it that after his victory over the Bulgarian army in 1014, the Byzantine Emperor Basil II blinded all 20,000 captured soldiers, leaving one one-eyed warrior of every hundred to lead them back to their king. For this, the Byzantine emperor earned the grim nickname "the Bulgar Slayer." The Bulgarian king died of a broken heart three days after he met his blinded army, and Bulgarian nationalist passions ignite each time tensions rise between Greeks and Bulgarians. In 1018 the Byzantine Empire conquered the weakened Bulgarian kingdom.

The Second Bulgarian Kingdom (1185–1396)

One hundred and sixty-seven years later the noble Bulgarian brothers Assen and Peter (later Kings Assen I and Peter) organized an uprising that overthrew Byzantine rule and laid the foundations of the Second Bulgarian Kingdom. It existed for about two hundred years, during which internal instability and external dangers were its most characteristic features. In addition to its eternal enemy, the Byzantine Empire, and the Magyars relentlessly attacking from the

The Battle of Nicopolis miniature, painted in 1596 (artist unknown).

northwest, Bulgaria faced a new, abominable enemy—the Crusaders.

When the Western Crusaders took Constantinople in 1204 and pronounced the Bulgarians their vassals, King Kaloyan, younger brother of Assen and Peter, couldn't bear the humiliation. At the battle of Adrianople his lightning-fast cavalry dealt the heavily armored knights a formidable blow, and he took their leader, Baldwin of Flanders, hostage, imprisoning him in a tower in the royal palace in Veliko Tarnovo. The tower carries his name and the sad story of his treason—his supposed attempt to seduce Kaloyan's wife. According to the legend, Baldwin was sentenced to fall to his death from a rock jutting over the deep river valley below.

Bulgaria enjoyed a second golden age under the reign of Ivan Asen II, who demonstrated not only brilliant military and strategic skills by destroying the Despot of Epirus, Theodore Angelus Comnenus, at Klokotniza in 1230, but also his exceptional talents as a diplomat. Thanks to his marriage to the Magyar princess Anna Maria, and the subsequent marriage to his archenemy Comnenus' daughter Irina, his five daughters and one son married into the royal families of Serbia, Russia, and Nicaea, thus providing peace and adding lands to the Bulgarian kingdom.

Tsar Ivan Asen II, ruler from 1218 to 1241.

Military victories and successful diplomacy brought the Second Bulgarian Kingdom to the height of its political dominance and territorial expansion—the Black Sea to the east, the Aegean to the south, and the Adriatic to the west. Commerce, culture, and the arts flourished once again, and masterpieces were born: before the early Italian Renaissance gave the world Giotto, Zograph Vasili and his apprentice Dimitar created the magnificent, lifelike frescoes in the Boyana Church, named a World Heritage Site in 1979.

In the fourteenth century, however, an ominous shadow was looming over the Balkans. The Ottoman Empire of the Oghuz Turks was vying for power in the peninsula, and by 1360 had captured important centers such as Bursa and Adrianople. Its crucial victory over the Serbian army at Kosovo Pole and the battle at Nicopolis in 1396 marked the fall of the Balkan

35

Peninsula into Ottoman hands, and Bulgaria remained a part of the Ottoman Empire for almost five hundred years, until 1878.

Bulgaria under Ottoman Rule

Being the first European territories to be captured by the Ottoman armies, the Balkans served as their base for expansion further west for the better part of two hundred years. The fall of Constantinople in 1453 marked the complete subjugation of Bulgaria to Ottoman rule. Theocratic by nature, the Ottoman administration was founded on a religious basis. A year after the fall of Constantinople, the populations of the Ottoman Empire were divided according to their faith. Each separate religious community, the so-called millet, was allowed to manage its own internal affairs. The millet system was an indication of religious tolerance in the Empire, but it also showed that the imperial administrators did not recognize that all Orthodox Christians were not Greeks, and that Serbs and Bulgarians had their own national churches with distinctive rituals and artistic expression. As a result, Bulgarians became the inferior group within the Orthodox millet, dominated by Greeks for centuries. The Bulgarians were also subjected to pressure to convert to Islam because their lands were more densely populated by Muslims and comprised part of the defensive belt surrounding Constantinople. They experienced both voluntary and forced conversion.

At the time, most of the Bulgarian population lived in self-run villages. Later, this experience of self-administration would be very helpful for the rebirth and revival of Bulgarian national consciousness.

The centuries of Ottoman rule saw most of Bulgaria's indigenous cultural centers—Veliko Tarnovo, churches, and monasteries—destroyed and Bulgarian revolts brutally suppressed, followed by the exodus of refugees seeking shelter in faraway lands.

Bulgarian National Revival and Struggles for Independence

"Of all the Slav peoples the Bulgarians were the most glorious; they were the first who called themselves tsars, the first to have a patriarch, the first to adopt the Christian faith, and it was they who conquered the largest expanse of territory. Thus, of all the Slav peoples, they were the strongest and the most honored, and the first Slav saints cast their radiance from amongst the Bulgarian people and through the Bulgarian language . . . Oh, Bulgarian, know your own ancestry and language, and study in your own tongue."

FATHER PAISII OF HILENDAR, 1762

These stirring words from *The Slavonic Bulgarian History of the Peoples, Tsars, Saints and of all their Deeds and of the Bulgarian Way of Life* are imprinted in the heart and mind of every Bulgarian. This book marked the awakening of the nation from a centuries-long slumber. New times were coming.

The creation of a regular conscript Ottoman army and the dissolution of the old feudal *sipahi* landowning system brought prosperity to the new middle classes, who benefited from the provisioning of the army. They in turn engaged in charitable activities such as building civic buildings, donating to monasteries, and investing into the education of the young generation, so becoming an important part of the Bulgarian national revival. By the mid-1800s growing numbers of Bulgarians went abroad to be educated, the first secular educational institution had been founded, followed by many others, and most Bulgarian communities had their own school teaching in their native language.

The spread of education laid the foundations of the Bulgarian intelligentsia—the driving force behind the struggle for an independent Bulgarian Church and, later, for political independence. In 1870, the Sultan officially pronounced the Bulgarian Church a separate exarchate, and it became a leading force in dealings with the authorities as well as a major sponsor of the community schools. From this moment on, the three most important public figures in each Bulgarian community became the mayor (*kmet*), the teacher (*daskal*), and the priest (*pop*).

The next aspiration of the Bulgarian intelligentsia became the achievement of political independence, as neighboring Greece and Serbia had done decades before. From its base in Romania, the Bulgarian Revolutionary Central Committee planned an armed national uprising. Within the country, the revolutionary leader and national hero Vasil Levski set up the Internal Revolutionary Organization, and created a network of secret regional cells to buy arms and train volunteers. Levski was captured and hanged by the Ottoman authorities, and the 1876 April Uprising was suppressed with great brutality.

The harshness with which the Ottomans crushed the revolt caught the attention of Western Europe: Bulgaria's fate had finally become a European concern. An international conference in Constantinople came up with proposals to the Sultan for reforms; the proposals were rejected, and Russia declared war on Turkey unilaterally soon after.

The Russo–Turkish War of 1877–78 and the concluding Peace Treaty of San Stefano marked the beginning of Bulgaria's liberation from Ottoman rule. The treaty provided for an autonomous Bulgarian state almost as large as the First Bulgarian Kingdom, stretching between the Black Sea and the Aegean. However, Britain and the Austro–Hungarian Empire stopped short of approving the San Stefano stipulations, as they felt that this might be an easy way for Imperial Russia to extend its influence over the Balkans altogether, through their Slavic and/or Orthodox Christian populations.

Four months later, in Berlin, a new treaty was signed.

It returned Macedonia and southern Thrace to the Ottomans. Eastern Rumelia (northern Thrace) was to remain within the borders of the Ottoman Empire but with a Bulgarian governor. The Treaty delivered a severe blow to the hopes of large populations of Bulgarians who remained outside the new independent Bulgarian state in Macedonia, Rumelia, and southern Thrace. For the next sixty years the Macedonian issue, created by the Berlin Treaty, would tear apart the Bulgarians and the other Balkan nations, bringing destruction to millions of people during fiercely suppressed revolts, two Balkan wars, and acts of hostility between Serbia, Macedonia, Greece, and Bulgaria. The reunification of Bulgarians remained a core national doctrine of the state until the middle of the twentieth century.

The Third Bulgarian Kingdom

> *"The Balkans produce more history*
> *than they can consume."*
> WINSTON CHURCHILL

Despite the anger and disappointment with the unfair decisions of the Berlin Treaty, a new Bulgarian state—a principality with a Christian prince to be elected by Bulgarians and approved by the Great Powers—was born in 1879. The first few decades of its existence would turn out to be some of the most turbulent and dynamic years of modern-day Bulgaria.

Alexander of Battenberg—a German noble connected to the Russian throne—was approved by the Grand National Assembly and became Prince (*knyaz*) of the Principality of Bulgaria. It took the new state seven years to unify the Principality with Eastern Rumelia, against the will of Russia. The unification created a major diplomatic crisis. Greece and Serbia demanded compensation for the loss of land and people, and while the Greeks were contained, the Serbs declared war on the newly created union between Bulgaria and Rumelia. The Bulgarians dealt the Serbian army a massive blow at Slivnitsa in November 1885, and only the diplomatic intervention of Austro–Hungary stopped their march on Belgrade.

More than anything, the battle at Slivnitsa bonded the Bulgarians north and south of Stara Planina into one single nation. The abdication of Prince Alexander Battenberg was the price paid for Russia to recognize the union. Stefan Stambolov, a Russian-educated liberal, became prime minister in 1887 and found a German prince—Ferdinand Saxe-Coburg-Gotha—to accept the Bulgarian throne. Stambolov mistrusted Russian intentions, and diplomatic relations remained quite frigid for the next ten years.

Independence brought drastic changes to Bulgaria. Industrialization set in motion the creation of a new class of laborers, and harsh working conditions pushed the new urban proletariat toward socialist ideas, which paved the way to the establishment in 1891 of the Social Democratic Party—a formation that gave

birth to the Bulgarian Communist Party, the oldest
Communist party in the world.

For the next fifty-five years the country fought in three
regional and two world wars; its political life was marked
by coups, assassinations, and social upheaval; and slowly
but surely it became the pariah of the Balkans, despite the
claims of British diplomacy that "the key to the situation
on the Balkans lies in Sofia," and "to approach any Balkan
problem without taking Bulgaria into account is merely
to deal with the periphery and to ignore what has so often
provided in the past to be the central core." Bulgaria twice
made the wrong choice—siding with the Central Powers
during the First World War and with the Axis during
the Second.

The Second World War

It had not been an easy decision to join the Axis. King
Boris had refused offers and advances from Germany,
Italy, and the Soviet Union in 1940. The Soviets had
offered Thrace to the Bulgarians, but reserved passage
through the Dardanelles and the right to use Bulgarian
naval bases on the Black Sea for themselves. This was
familiar rhetoric, however. Boris knew that they had
called this configuration "a Soviet security zone" and
applied it to the Baltic States before incorporating
them into the USSR. In December 1940 pressure from
Germany increased, and on March 2, 1941, Bulgaria
allowed the German army to enter Bulgarian territory en
route to Greece. After the National Assembly declared

King Boris III ruled from 1918—after the abdication of his father, Ferdinand I—until his death in 1943.

war on the United States and Great Britain, the King disappeared and was found deep in prayer in the St. Alexander Nevski Cathedral. Bulgaria had reached the point of no return.

In the subsequent months and years, the country stood by its Axis allies, but King Boris was anxious when it came to German demands in the military sphere. He didn't want to deploy the Bulgarian army beyond the Balkans and succeeded in getting German consent to keep it in the region against a possible Turkish invasion, a move that ensured his popularity at home. Though Germany's ally, Bulgaria also never declared war on the USSR.

In 1943 an agreement between Bulgaria and Germany required the former to send Bulgaria's 50,000 Jews to Nazi extermination camps. Thanks to the efforts of the Bulgarian Orthodox Church, members of the National Assembly, and broad public opposition, not a single Bulgarian Jew was deported. However, heavy legal restrictions were placed on Bulgaria's Jews and, despite public opposition, 20,000 of Sofia's Jews were expelled to the provinces, their properties confiscated, and men sent to work in labor camps. In addition, Bulgarian forces rounded up and deported some 11,300 Jews to Nazi extermination camps from occupied areas of Greek Thrace and Yugoslav Macedonia and Pirot.

On August 14, 1943, Hitler summoned King Boris to a meeting in Germany. Two weeks later the King succumbed to a mysterious illness. While the true cause of his sudden illness and subsequent death remains unknown, popular rumor claims that he was poisoned by Hitler for not deporting Bulgaria's Jews, as well as for his refusal to send troops to the eastern front or to declare war on Soviet Russia, as had been required for all of Germany's other allies.

Bulgaria had never before witnessed a funeral ceremony like the one organized for King Boris at

St. Alexander Nevski Cathedral. The body was taken to the Rila Monastery, and weeping crowds lined the entire route of the solemn procession. After the Communist takeover of Bulgaria in 1944, the zinc coffin with the royal remains was secretly exhumed and buried in the courtyard of the Vrana Palace, then much later removed again to an unknown location. Only the King's heart was found in Vrana; in 1993 his widow took it back to Rila Monastery.

On September 5, 1944, the Soviet Union declared war on Bulgaria. Within days the Soviets were crossing the Danube and being met with joy by ordinary Bulgarians who were thankful to see the Germans fleeing the country and Russian soldiers coming to their aid again. The Communist-backed Fatherland Front formed a new coalition government led by Kimon Georgiev, and a month later joined the Allies and fought through Hungary and Austria with the Red Army's Third Ukrainian Front. Thirty-two thousand Bulgarian soldiers lost their lives in the campaign. Following the defeat of the Axis Powers, Communism emerged as the dominant political force and Bulgaria became the staunchest Eastern European ally of the Soviet Union for the next forty-five years.

King Boris's son Simeon and his family were forced into exile as Communist control over Bulgaria increased, and a referendum on September 15, 1946, overwhelmingly chose a republican path of development for the country.

The Question of Macedonia

In 1944, the exiled Bulgarian Communist leader Georgi Dimitrov and Joseph Tito of Yugoslavia started negotiating the creation of a Federation of the Southern Slavs, which included the incorporation of Macedonia as a separate unified entity. Bulgaria encouraged the inhabitants of the Blagoevgrad region adjacent to Macedonia to claim Macedonian identity. This scheme soon came to grief, blocked by Stalin's desire to control the new Eastern bloc, and by differences over the national character and status of the Macedonians. The Macedonian issue has created even worse problems in the twenty-first century, particularly over the issues of language, history, and ethnic minorities. Macedonian is not recognized as a separate language by the Bulgarian Academy of Science and is considered a regional southwestern dialect of Bulgarian—something the citizens of North Macedonia fiercely reject and oppose. At the same time, Bulgarians argue North Macedonia has been appropriating parts of Bulgarian history—including historical figures and events—and representing them as Macedonian history. Finally, Bulgarians living in North Macedonia are not recognized as minorities.

Zhivkov's Bulgaria: The Communist Years

For generations of Bulgarians, Communism has a face—the face of Todor Zhivkov, who was not only the longest-serving leader of any of the socialist

Todor Zhivkov in Berlin, 1971.

countries, but one of the longest-ruling non-royals in history. Born in 1911, he joined the Communist Party youth branch when he was seventeen. A poor peasant's son, but highly ambitious and politically savvy, he got a job at the state printing shop in Sofia, and three years later gained full membership of the Party. Actively involved in anti-fascist activities during the Second World War, he became the deputy commander of the Sofia operations area of the anti-German and anti-monarchist partisan movement. Years later, under his rule, many of his fellow combatants rose to prominent Party and government positions.

The Communist Party dominated the Fatherland Front—the political coalition that took power in September 1944—and propelled Zhivkov to political stardom right after September 9, 1944. First, he became

The Largo, or Independence Square, in Sofia, Built in the 1950s, it's an example of Socialist Classicism architecture and formely housed the Communist Party headquaters.

the head of the Sofia police force and was elected candidate member of the Central Committee of the Communist Party less than a year later. Then, in 1948, he became a full member, and just three years later became a full member of the Politburo of the BCP, and was responsible for countering resistance to forced farm collectivization. In 1954 the hardline Stalinist Vulko Chervenkov was removed from his post of General Secretary of the Politburo of BCP, under Soviet pressure after Stalin's demise, and Zhivkov took his place. This was the beginning of decades of uncontested rule, which saw political opposition obliterated, agriculture collectivized, industry nationalized, the Orthodox Church state-controlled, and many of its members turned into agents of the then secret police, the Committee for State Security (CSS).

Mirroring the Soviet rejection of Stalinism and the personality cult, the BCP convened a Central Committee Plenary Meeting in April 1956, and it was at that plenum that Zhivkov became de facto leader of the country. By pointing the finger at Chervenkov first, and then at Prime Minister Yugov in 1962 and replacing him as prime minister, Zhivkov strengthened his positions to an extent that he became the undisputed one and only political leader of Bulgaria for nearly the entirety of the country's existence as an independent republic. In 1971, constitutional changes allowed Zhivkov to assume one more post—of head of state, or Chairman of the State Council. As of this moment, political, executive, and state power were concentrated in the hands of one man—Comrade Todor Zhivkov.

During his thirty-five years at the helm of the country, Zhivkov remained absolutely loyal to his Soviet allies. However, he felt that a more liberal rule would guarantee him popularity. And indeed, his PR agents created a "Man of the People" image that would subsequently be promoted by state-run media for years. His down-to-earth behavior, his love of jokes, and even his nickname "Tato" (Pop, or Dad) were his signature of a self-made man who never forgot where he came from. His rule marked a period of unprecedented political and economic stability for Bulgaria. By the mid-1950s real salaries rose 57 percent, universal health care was introduced, and 1957 saw collective farm workers benefit from the first agricultural pension and welfare system in Eastern Europe. Yet, a centrally managed economic model could not perform well in the long term. The 1970s saw stagnation, and an attempt at reviving the economy by the introduction of a new Economic Model was made in 1981, but its effects were short-lived and unsatisfactory.

Four years later the reformist Soviet leader Mikhail Gorbachev visited Sofia and urged Zhivkov to make Bulgaria more economically competitive. Bulgarian-style perestroika followed. In January 1989 Decree 56 was introduced: it was a fundamental departure from the principles of socialist economy as it allowed private citizens to own companies and have employees. But the hourglass of Zhivkov's rule was running out. Ten months later sweeping social and political changes in Eastern Europe ousted him.

The Turkish Exodus

In December 1984, Zhivkov had instigated a campaign of forceful assimilation of Bulgaria's Turkish minority, by obliging ethnic Turks to change from Turkish to Bulgarian names. There was serious resistance to this policy. In May 1989, Zhivkov suddenly granted permission to all Turks to leave the country, and over 300,000 crossed the Turkish border within three months. This was the beginning of the end for the longtime leader as Bulgaria became the target of unanimous criticism from the international community. Even the Soviets objected. Gorbachev had already given up on Zhivkov as an inflexible old-school hardliner, and he gave the green light to younger Bulgarian Communist Party functionaries to oust him. Taken by surprise, Zhivkov tried to retaliate, but it was too late. The seventy-eight-year-old man of the people resigned on November 10, 1989.

Post-Communism and Its Discontents

November 10, 1989 brought shock and then ecstasy to the nation. And it wasn't just the downfall of a man whom Bulgarians simply couldn't imagine giving up power in the way he did. Something much more important happened on this day. The Berlin Wall came down, signaling the beginning of a new era. Bulgarians remained glued to their TVs during the bloody Romanian Christmas, watching Zhivkov's best friend Ceausescu and his wife Elena face a firing squad. Mass protests erupted and thousands of people took to the streets in the freezing December of 1989. Everyone wanted change for the better—a better life, more freedom, a voice in the internal affairs of the country. Exhilaration was the word that described the feelings of Bulgarians at the time. Little did they imagine that twenty-two years later they would take to the streets one more time with the same demands.

June 1990 saw the first multiparty elections since the Communist takeover of the country. The ruling

Communist Party reinvented itself, becoming the Bulgarian Socialist Party. There was no time for an organized democratic political force to stand against it, and the Socialists got themselves an easy election victory. Strong social unrest and the passage of a new constitution marked the rest of the year; then the first fully democratic parliamentary elections were held in 1991, won by a loose alliance called the Union of Democratic Forces (UDF). The first direct presidential elections were held the next year.

The transitional period to democracy and a market economy threw Bulgaria into a period of social and economic agony that climaxed in a stark economic and financial crisis during the last months of 1996 and the beginning of 1997. The country experienced hyperinflation that was unheard of. Despite this, the elections of May 1997 returned the UDF to power, and then Prime Minister Ivan Kostov introduced a series of reforms that helped to stabilize the economy. His government also initiated the application for Bulgaria's membership in NATO.

The rule of the UDF brought about long-delayed economic reforms, including large-scale privatization of state-owned enterprises and the beginning of long-sought talks for accession to the European Union. However, his management methods were quite controversial and highly criticized, and corruption ran rampant. His political opponents blamed him for the sellout of large state-owned enterprises for pennies.

Public opinion also took a negative turn because of the unpopular financial reforms, and the UDF lost to a coalition led by, ironically, the man who had been sent into exile fifty-five years before.

In July 2001, Bulgaria's ex-king, Simeon Saxe-Coburg-Gotha, became prime minister, the first former monarch in post-Communist Eastern Europe to do so. Under his National Movement for Stability and Progress government Bulgaria joined the North Atlantic Treaty Organization on March 29, 2004. It continued to pursue democratic reform and development of a market economy as well as membership in the European Union. These were another four controversial years. The former king brought technocrats and Western-educated yuppies to run the country: they might have been competent, but they never won the confidence of the Bulgarian people. Simeon's well-advertised promises for a brighter future and higher standard of living never materialized. Disappointment led to electoral losses for him in 2005, and political disaster in 2009 when his party got just 3 percent of the votes and no seats in parliament. Shortly after, he resigned his posts and left the country, having reclaimed the family's properties nationalized by the Communists. Rumor had it that this was the only reason he had returned.

This same disappointment brought the Bulgarian Socialist Party back to power. Following the June 2005 general elections, Sergei Stanishev became the new prime minister of a coalition government on August 16, 2005. The Stanishev government continued Bulgaria's cooperation with the Euro-Atlantic countries and its close partnership with the United States. Bulgaria became an active partner in coalition operations in Afghanistan as well as in UN-led peacekeeping operations in the Balkans. It also joined the European Union on January 1, 2007. Yet many failures like corruption scandals and the consequent freezing of EU funds marked the rule of the Socialists.

The July 2009 general elections witnessed the meteoric rise of a new formation, Citizens for the European Development of Bulgaria (GERB). It took 116 of 240 seats in parliament, and its leader Boyko Borisov, the former bodyguard of Todor Zhivkov and Simeon Saxe-Coburg-Gotha, became prime minister. Borisov formed a minority government, but, in the course of its second year in office, his coalition partners gradually withdrew their support for the GERB. The austerity measures the government had to take in the aftermath of the global financial crisis led to massive unrest and Borisov's government resigned in 2013, leaving the Socialists to form a coalition government headed by a non-partisan prime minister, Plamen Oresharski.

Oresharski's cabinet was short-lived for a number of reasons: it introduced unpopular policies and provoked a wave of mass protests because of the non-transparent appointment of a compromised individual to head the State Agency of National Security (ДАНС). The coalition dissolved, and, in the aftermath of the cabinet's resignation, Borisov won both the 2014 and 2017 general elections and formed two consecutive cabinets. His style of government and the subsequent system-wide corruption attributed to his rule brought about huge social unrest and mass protests on the streets and squares of the country in the summer of 2020. Borisov didn't cave in despite the numerous failures of his cabinet and his botched management of the Covid-19 crisis, but he lost at the next elections in April 2021.

The year of 2021 was another tumultuous year for Bulgarian politics. It took a total of three elections for a government to be formed, as no single party was able to secure a majority of votes or form a coalition. By the third round of elections, voter turnout was at an all-time low of 33.7 percent. Two caretaker cabinets appointed by President Radev governed in the interim and won widespread support for their stance against corruption and for maintaining fair elections. A new coalition government was eventually formed in November by a new political alliance consisting of We Continue the Change (ПП), the Bulgarian Socialist Party, There's Such People (ИТН), and Democratic Bulgaria. During the first months of coming to power, Premier Petkov and his cabinet were faced with one crisis after another—the ongoing Covid-19 pandemic, a sluggish economy, rising energy prices, and urgent foreign policy issues, among them Russia's invasion of Ukraine.

In 2022 Petkov's government took a stance against Russia by refusing to pay for Russian gas in rubles, and subsequently declared seventy Russian diplomats persona non grata on charges of spying. GERB accused Petkov of jeopardizing the country's financial stability, citing incompetence in the energy sector and spiraling inflation. A vote of no-confidence saw the collapse of Petkov's government and the country thrown into its fourth round of elections in under two years. At the time of writing, the November 2022 election results had not yet been announced, but the deep divisions that have characterized the political landscape in recent years are likely to remain influential.

Upon becoming members of NATO and the EU, Bulgarians had been filled with hope and readily accepted European principles and norms. Yet in 2022 Bulgaria remained the poorest country of the Union. According to the National Statistical Institute of Bulgaria in 2021, 532,400 Bulgarians (22.1 percent of the population) were living below the poverty line, defined as a monthly average of 504.33 leva, or 250 euros, per person. The economic and political hardships experienced since joining have trampled the initial optimism and Bulgarians are no longer unanimous: today there are Eurosceptics across the political spectrum. The armed conflict between Russia and Ukraine that began in 2022 further divided the country into Russophiles and Russophobes pushing for pro-military involvement.

COVID-19 IN BULGARIA

In March 2020 Bulgaria closed its borders to international travelers: Covid-19 had arrived. During the first months of the pandemic the number of infected Bulgarians was relatively low, but the measures Borisov's government took in response were heavy-handed. Strict lockdowns were enforced, as was a 28-day-long quarantine for those who tested positive for the virus. Medical professionals were divided. On the one hand, there were the official representatives who daily announced statistics of those infected, dying, or dead, which seemed only to add to people's fear of the virus. On the other hand, there were medical professionals who vocally warned against the negative effects of lockdowns and measures that seemed to scare the population while doing little to protect or educate people. Overall, the population was largely supportive of the measures, and according to a UN poll in 2021, a majority of Bulgarians were actually supportive of harsher measures.

The authorities' handling of the crisis played into the public's long-standing mistrust of government and as a result, many Bulgarians refused to get vaccinated. People's apprehensiveness incurred a heavy price: by late 2021 Bulgaria had the second highest Covid mortality rate in the world—403 in 100,000—according to Agence France-Presse. By April 1, 2022, when all remaining restrictions were lifted, only 31 percent of the population had been double vaccinated. Thankfully, despite the low vaccine uptake, the country's healthcare system proved itself competent and though there were instances of shortages, an acute crisis never developed. Medical staff were financially supported, as were pensioners and some businesses.

THE ECONOMY

In the past, the major industrial sectors of Bulgaria were agriculture, metallurgy, chemicals, and machine manufacture. Westerners, however, may be more familiar with Bulgaria's inexpensive and delicious wines, its dark and aromatic tobaccos, and its rose attar, an essential oil for perfume, the country's oldest industry. Today's leading industries include IT and telecommunications, agriculture, industry, pharmaceuticals, textiles, retail, and tourism. Bulgaria is also finding new avenues of national revenue: in 2020 a new pipeline, Balkan Stream, became operational, supplying Russian gas to Europe, Turkey, and others via Bulgaria. This is set to provide the economy with hundreds of millions of dollars annually in transfer fees and brought much needed investment to its domestic energy infrastructure. It also saw Bulgaria secure its position as a regional player with leverage.

As in other countries, the Covid-19 pandemic served a blow to Bulgaria's economy, yet stability was maintained. Unemployment reached highs of 6.1 percent in April 2021—approximately half the rate experienced during the 2008 economic crisis—and by the end of Q2 2022, had recovered to 4.7 percent. Certain companies, like pharmaceuticals, supermarket chains, online vendors, and delivery providers saw an increase in business and, despite pandemic-related restrictions and supply chain issues, the economy grew by 4.1 percent overall in 2021.

In the aftermath of the pandemic, the EU implemented an ambitious recovery and resilience plan, and Bulgaria submitted its national plan worth over six billion euros, which was approved in April 2022. The plan provides for more than a hundred investment projects in the energy sector, business, infrastructure, and education.

Stable and with a solid banking system, Bulgaria has become an increasingly popular outsourcing location. Giants such as Boeing, BMW, General Motors, Siemens, and Nortel employ Bulgarian IT companies. The relatively inexpensive and highly qualified labor force, along with low business taxes and office rental costs, are attractive to investors.

Before the pandemic hit, tourism was another fast-developing industry and is expected to recover in line with global trends. The country's geographic location provides perfect climatic conditions for year-round activities from skiing to scuba diving.

Plans to join the Eurozone in 2011 fell through as a result of the euro sovereign debt crisis and is now projected to take place in 2024. Over a million Bulgarians are thought to be employed throughout the EU.

CHAPTER TWO

VALUES & ATTITUDES

THE BULGARIAN WORLDVIEW

Three major factors determine a nation's character. The socio-historical factor is embedded in its history—its destiny, the wars it fought, and the time social classes were born and started developing. The geographical factor is the unique mix of territory, landforms, natural resources, climate, and economy, and the people's relationships with these features. The cultural and educational factor involves the spiritual dimension—the predominant religion, customs and traditions, mythology, folklore, and literature, as well as the general level of education.

Bulgarians have had a complicated and dramatic history. Under Ottoman rule they suffered arrested development in the social, political, cultural, and educational spheres of life for five hundred years. Yet, the roller coaster of events in the last one hundred and fifty years have had little influence upon their national character and worldview.

Bulgarians are, first and foremost, very pragmatic. For centuries they have had to rely on their own devices to survive; they developed complete self-reliance, resourcefulness, and acumen—their most characteristic features—as well as curiosity about the surrounding world and the universe as a whole, receptivity, and, last but not least, a strong sense of humor. At the same time, centuries of foreign oppression gave birth to servility, distrust, corruptibility, xenomania, and criticism of everything and everybody. It was during these dark times that Bulgarians completely lost respect for authority—a national trait that endures to this day.

The Bulgarian survival instinct has led to a widespread belief that conformity is always the better policy. This pragmatic rationale is behind such expressions as "If you don't trouble trouble, trouble won't trouble you." Bulgarian individualism is perfectly reflected in the popular saying "A wolf's neck is strong because the wolf takes care of his own business." Partnership and teamwork are fine, but if you want to succeed you should rely solely on yourself. Among the most valued personal qualities is ingenuity: "His wit is so sharp it can split the thread in two and sew trousers for the flea." The industrious are respected, but those who tend to be boastful show-offs are duly reprimanded. "The hen that cackles most lays the least," Bulgarians like to say.

Blessed to be situated at the crossroads of East and West, Bulgaria has had to reflect hard and long upon its national character and choices after many national catastrophes. Modernity brings the pressing issue of globalization and the preservation of national identity. Despite overwhelming changes, Bulgarians believe they'll always be able to persevere because of their agility, flexibility, audacity, and determination.

FAMILY VALUES

Traditionally, Bulgarian society is family-oriented, and the extended family forms a tightly knit and highly dependable network of support. What can look like nepotism to people from meritocratic cultures is just the normal way of social functioning to a Bulgarian. As a matter of fact, the name of the phenomenon itself is impossible to translate into English, as it's a complex form, combining the words for "a brother-in-law of the husband" and "a brother-in-law of the wife" (*shurobadzhanashtina*). Some friendly advice: don't to try to pronounce it in front of a Bulgarian, because they'll never guess what you are trying to say! The importance of family relations is so great that there are more than two dozen words to describe all the different male and female relatives a person has.

Extended families maintain close relations at all times; they always come together at three important life events—family marriages, births, and deaths. It is considered highly disrespectful not to invite all your relatives to a wedding, or to miss informing them of the birth of your child or the passing of a parent or someone in your immediate family.

Bulgarian society is also patriarchal, with the eldest male family member making the final decision about all the important matters. This comes from the old times of the so-called family cooperative—a social grouping of up to twenty members led by the eldest and most respected male. The cooperative consisted of the parents, their adult sons, who brought their spouses into the cooperative after the marriage, and their children. If the parents' parents were still alive, they were also a highly respected part of the group. At times, four generations lived under the same roof, and each family member had a strictly determined role in everyday life. While men worked the fields, bred cattle and sheep, or traveled on business, women managed the household, grew and prepared food, made clothes, and raised the children. Husbands and wives functioned in tandem, sharing responsibilities and raising their children in a spirit of respect, honor, and hard work.

Although socialism introduced equality between men and women in all spheres of life, remnants of the old family cooperative can be observed in Bulgaria even today, especially in the villages and the smaller towns. Grandparents take an active part in raising their grandchildren. Children live with their parents until they marry; those who remain single live with their parents and take care of them. It is considered shameful to send an elderly parent to a nursing home. Instead, the adult children of old and ailing parents hire a nurse to take care of them while they are at work. This is why it is still deemed exceptionally important to get married and have children, even though new times bring new perceptions and attitudes to the institution of marriage and childbearing. Living together without being married—something unheard of just a few years ago—and postponing having babies to build a career first are slowly becoming the norm for young urbanites.

Visitors to Bulgaria shouldn't be surprised if one of the first questions he or she is asked is whether they are married and have any children. Bulgarian parents adore their children, feel immense pride in their achievements, and turn them into one of their favorite topics for discussion. There is also a strong relationship between the younger and the older generations.

THE ROLE OF WOMEN

> *"A house without a housewife is like a flock without a shepherd."*
> BULGARIAN SAYING

Bulgarian women have always played a very important role in the family and in society as a whole. They worked the fields whenever their fathers, brothers, husbands, and sons were away fighting wars. And there was no scarcity of wars; in sixty-six years (1879–1945) Bulgaria had fought three regional and two world wars, losing four of them. Because so many lives were lost, in 1938 married women and widows received the right to vote. Bulgarian women had demonstrated courage, drive, and audacity before the Liberation: they fought the Ottomans as *haiduts* (freedom fighters), the Maid Marians of the Balkans. A brave teacher, Rayna Knyaginia, embroidered the flag of the April Uprising in 1876. An incredible woman and mother of five revolutionaries, Baba (Granny) Tonka Obretenova, provided shelter to the revolutionary committee of Rousse, a large radical organization paving the way to Bulgarian liberation in the later part of the nineteenth century. Raina Kassabova, a volunteer nurse in a field hospital during the Balkan War of 1912–13, was the first woman in the world on board a combat aircraft. She was there to spread leaflets appealing to the enemy soldiers in Edirne to stop the bloodshed.

Women—teachers, poets, actresses, opera singers, and writers—became an important part of the post-liberation intelligentsia, too. It was only after the Communist takeover, however, that men and women were finally granted equal rights, and this saw Bulgarian women across society become active participants in all spheres of public life as professionals, politicians, academics, public figures, artists, and internationally known athletes. More women hold higher education degrees than men: in 2022 39.5 percent of women aged twenty-four to thirty-four had received a university education compared to 28 percent of men in the same age group.

Following the start of democratic changes in 1998, many women made names for themselves in politics, the media, and public life. The economist Reneta Indzova became the first female premier of the country. Miglena Kuneva began her political career as a European integration minister and went on to become a European commissioner for consumer protection. Nadezhda Mihailova held the post of foreign minister of Bulgaria, was elected to lead the Union of Democratic Forces, and became a member of the European Parliament in 2009. Irina Bokova is a Bulgarian politician and the former director general of UNESCO (2009–17). International Monetary Fund (IMF) managing director Kristalina Georgieva is another prominent Bulgarian, who headed the organization in 2019. Women have made inroads in business, too. They have been at the helm of the Bulgarian National Radio, Hewlett-Packard Bulgaria, as well as holding numerous positions in public office.

Bulgarian women are good at balancing their careers with their family obligations. They take pride in their home and their homemade dishes, so the typical wife will leave work, go shopping for fresh food, and then return home to cook a delicious dinner for her family. Most working women cannot afford help at home, so they are also responsible for keeping their homes in order. Women are in charge of entertaining guests at various family functions, too.

International Women's Day (March 8) celebrates women as professionals as well as mothers (there is no other Mother's Day in Bulgaria). Women are the center of attention for the day; foreign visitors will notice flowers and beautifully wrapped presents in every woman's hands. It is customary for colleagues to go out for a drink or dinner together after work to celebrate this special day, and the bill is always picked up by the men.

HOSPITALITY AND GENEROSITY

"Are Bulgarians hospitable? Yes, a lot. We prepare the most delicious dishes for our honored guests. We serve them our best brandies and finest wines in our most expensive crystal sets. We take out the silver cutlery. We make sure our guests go to bed stuffed to the gills and drunk! You can almost always go 'visiting' with someone you know and trust that you will be provided food, drink, and a free bed for the night. You can even stick around for a few days."
TIHOMIR DIMITROV, WRITER AND POET

Hospitality and generosity were deeply imbedded in

the Bulgarian understanding of morality during the centuries of living in the Ottoman Empire. To refuse to offer food, drink, or shelter to the traveler who reached a village after dark was equal to leaving him at the mercy of the elements, the beasts of nature, and the dark forces lurking outside. Hospitality is a traditional family value that children are taught from an early age as they observe their parents open their houses and pantries to friends and strangers alike. A poem by Dimiter Metodiev starts, "Please, Lord, let my house be on a crossroads so that anyone passing through will come to visit, share our bread, take food for the road, and leave us his words of gratitude and wishes for health."

For Bulgarians, hospitality and pride go together: pride in their home, the produce of their gardens, and the spirits and wine they make themselves, as well as pride in their dexterity and in the mastery of their spouse's culinary skills. When a foreign visitor is invited to a restaurant by a Bulgarian acquaintance or business partner, it goes without saying that the host will pick up the tab. If the invitee tries to share it, he or she will likely be told they can pay the bill "next time."

The offering of bread and salt (*hlyab i sol*) is a traditional Bulgarian custom expressing hospitality, showing that the guest is welcomed. The bread and salt are usually presented by a woman. Bulgarians make a certain type of flat, fancy, and decorated pita bread for this occasion. When presented with the pita, the guest is supposed to take a small piece, dip it into the salt, and eat it. This custom is common for all official visits, regardless of whether the guest is foreign or Bulgarian.

RELIGION

Bulgaria adopted Orthodox Christianity as the state religion in 864 CE under King Boris I, and today more than half of the population (59.4 percent) is Eastern Orthodox, although the constitution of the country does not call it an official religion—it defines it as "the traditional religion" of the country. The postwar socialist government made atheism the state doctrine, and according to the 2021 Census, 21.8 percent of the population is atheist. Minority groups represent Islam and Catholicism as well as some Eastern religions. The followers of the latter gather in groups and societies for esoteric knowledge, and readings and lectures are given to large audiences, various meditation and physical techniques are practiced, and lamas, priests, and preachers from all over the world come to teach in Bulgaria. Nevertheless, the majority of Bulgarians observe Christian traditions and more than half of them identify positively with Orthodox Christianity. The tendency to turn back to God and the Holy Book is getting stronger, boosted by the advent of democracy and the promotion of the centuries-old beliefs and values of the Bulgarian nation.

According to polls, the majority of Bulgarians believe that religion has a positive influence on society, and new churches, chapels, and monasteries continue to be constructed or rebuilt. Ancient icons, altars, and frescoes are being restored, and decrepit village churches are being renovated and opened again for believers. The publication of Christian literature has also increased, as has the demand for it.

The history of Bulgarian education is intrinsically linked to religion. From their inception in the fifteenth century until today, Bulgarian schools have taught not just literacy but Christian morals and values. These were at the core of the Bulgarian educational tradition. During Ottoman rule schools preserved the language and Christian faith of the population. With the growth of secular education in the Renaissance, religious training gradually became one subject taught under different names (Law of God, Catechism, Church history, or Liturgy), depending on the requirements of the school trustees and the training of the teachers.

All Bulgarian families celebrate the traditional Christian holidays. Name days, so-called after archangels, saints, and martyrs, have always been widely celebrated as well. This is a time of revival for Orthodoxy in Bulgaria.

REGIONALISM, PATRIOTISM, CHAUVINISM

If you were to ask the residents of Sofia to define themselves, they would probably say: first, a Sofianite, next a Bulgarian. Very few would answer "a citizen of the world," and even fewer "a European." Most certainly they would also say that they are very proud to be Bulgarians, no matter how hard life is or how discontented people are with the realities of present-day Bulgaria. These are the results of a recent sociological poll, which brings out the typical Bulgarian regionalism that takes precedence over EU membership and cosmopolitanism. Just an example: ever since Sofia won the privilege of becoming Bulgaria's capital in 1879, beating Plovdiv by a narrow margin, the citizens of the two Bulgarian cities have been involved in a bitter rivalry that borders, in some extreme cases, on bigotry.

Patriotism is deeply rooted in history; in fact, it is "the national mission," as the philosopher Hannah Arendt calls it. Patriotism has always been an integral part of the Bulgarian national identity. It was consciously promoted to boost courage and get people up in arms during times of conflict and wars, of which Bulgarians have faced many. But it was also needed for ideological reasons, such as to counter passivity and pessimism. One person was particularly responsible for an immense outburst of patriotism during the 1970s. She was Lyudmila Zhivkova, daughter of Party and State leader Todor Zhivkov. As minister of culture, Zhivkova promoted a cultural policy heavily focused on national identity and excessive national pride. She was behind the idea of a grand celebration in 1981 called "Thirteen Centuries Bulgaria" and the International Children's Assembly

"Banner of Peace," first held in 1979. So, as the polls show, even today the majority of Bulgarians are bigger patriots than they are Europeans or citizens of the world (despite the 2 million plus Bulgarians who have emigrated during the last two decades!).

There is a very thin line between patriotism and chauvinism in the Balkans, even in the twenty-first century. Bulgaria has mostly followed a rational foreign policy after the the introduction of democracy; however, the picture changes somewhat when it comes to regional Balkan politics. "Greater Bulgaria" chauvinism reappeared on the political scene when the country used its right to veto the setting of a date for the opening of talks with Macedonia on its accession to the European Union. Bulgaria was the first country to recognize the Republic of Macedonia in 1992, yet generally Bulgarians do not recognize the separate existence of a Macedonian language or, indeed, a Macedonian nation. The language is considered a dialect of Bulgarian, and the people living in the territory of today's Macedonia an offshoot of the Bulgarian people. In a nutshell, the Macedonian question continues to present a burning issue in the Balkans.

ATTITUDES TOWARD OTHERS

Generally speaking, Bulgarian society is more collectivist than individualist, although this has started to change, especially among the younger generations.

"Privacy" is a foreign word without an equivalent in Bulgarian. It is loosely translated as "personal space," but it's a brand-new addition to the language, together with many other neologisms directly appropriated from English. Family, relatives, and close friends belong to the same group and are offered preferential treatment. This may sound like cronyism to many outsiders, but it's a long-established trait that can still be observed in Bulgarian society today. People outside the group are treated with indifference and even suspicion. This group identification nurtures a strong "us versus them" mentality and, as some have pointed out, provides fertile ground for stereotyping of others, and even racism.

There is no better example of this than the existence of a nationalist formation, the ATAKA Party, which attracted 24 percent of the votes at the 2009 elections with the promise of "Bulgaria for Bulgarians." ATAKA and its leader were vocal opponents of the integration of Bulgarian minorities—Roma and Bulgarian Turks—into the national milieu. Its successor, *Vazrazhdane* (Revival), took part in all three 2021 elections, and won thirteen seats in the National Assembly in November. Polls predict an increase in the parliamentary seats for nationalists in the fall 2022 general elections. Its leader is both a Eurosceptic and anti-NATO who, when Ukraine was attacked by Russia, organized protests against Bulgarian solidarity with Ukraine.

WORK ETHIC

"A job done hastily brings shame to its craftsman."
"Work is not a rabbit; it won't run away."
BULGARIAN SAYINGS

The Bulgarian work ethic is hard to sum up—the situation is complex! First of all, there is a clear distinction between working for oneself and one's family, and working for others, be they employers or clients. Working hard for oneself or one's family is a given for most Bulgarians and it is taken for granted that it is both required and expected. Yet decades of living under communism, where people worked for low, fixed salaries, no matter how hard or how little one worked, heavily influenced the work ethic of the postwar socialist state generations. Those who lived under communism also had absolutely no economic incentive or opportunity to use their own initiative and resourcefulness in a business of their own, and so many adopted a behavioral pattern known as "learned helplessness," a psychological term that describes the apathy brought about by the impossibility of being an agent of change, resulting in leaving decision-making and initiative to an authority figure.

Another important factor when considering attitudes to work is age. Older generations of Bulgarians who began their careers under socialism considered work to be the epitome of self-realization, while younger

Bulgarians for the most part seek fulfillment not in labor but in its fruits—i.e. in what money can buy. Somewhat suprisingly, in a recent survey only 15 percent of young Bulgarians said hard work was the key to financial success, while 71 percent did not believe one could become rich by working hard, a sign that communist mentalities remain influential in this area.

ATTITUDES TOWARD TIME

Language reveals a lot about a culture's attitude to time. For Bulgarians, any hasty reaction would almost always lead to a mistake or a wrong decision, so they love to take their time. Consider the following expressions, which one hears very often in Bulgaria: "Haste makes waste." "Hasty climbers have sudden falls." "The more haste, the less speed." "Stop running like a calf in front of its mother."

If there is one thing that annoys foreigners who are living or working in Bulgaria, it's the Bulgarian sense of time and punctuality. Bulgarians may show up as much as an hour later than an agreed-upon time. Sometimes it's not just about appointments, but the reliability of what they say as well. A Bulgarian may invite you for lunch, promising to call two days later to let you know the venue, but may arrive on the day of the meeting without having contacted you at all. As in the West, you will often hear people say, "We should meet for a drink soon," but it doesn't mean much, being just a form of self-perceived politeness. Foreigners who come from monochronic (sequential) cultures, who are used to doing one thing at a time, understandably feel frustrated, because Bulgarian culture is polychronic— fitting in other things as they occur. This way of dealing with time is associated with knowledge from the past that provides valuable experience for similar situations in the present or the future, and is negotiated on a daily basis. Bulgarians attach great importance to emotional contact among people, rather than to social norms and regulations. In practice this means that they will spend as much time as it takes to build a relationship rather than look at their watch every now and then. In one of his letters the Bulgarian national hero Vasil Levski wrote: "We are in Time, and Time is in us; we change Time, and Time changes us." It is in the Bulgarian character to treat time as an equal, not as a master.

INDIVIDUALISM AND COLLECTIVISM

"A united troop can move mountains."
"Fend for yourself."
BULGARIAN SAYINGS

Bulgarians are a baffling mix of individualism and collectivism—the result of complex historical, political, and social transformations. This mix started with the specific social and economic structure established under Ottoman rule: separated according to their religious identity, Ottoman subjects were left to self-manage their agricultural and artisanal communities, dominated by traditional patriarchal values. These values of diligence, patriotism, frugality, solidarity, good neighborliness, and hospitality were a guarantee for the preservation of Bulgarian national identity.

The ideology and policies of the Socialist period brought about the destruction of this traditional cultural world, yet utilized and built upon the industriousness and the collectivist vein of the national psyche.

The 1990s brought drastic changes to life once more. Following forty-five years of socialist rule, neoliberal capitalism and new information technologies set the stage for a consumerist society.

Today, young Bulgarians are just like other young people in the developed world—they're Internet-savvy, enjoy Western pop culture, speak foreign languages, and feel at home in Miami, Madrid, or Milan.

Visitors to the country will see ample evidence of the collectivist mindset once they leave the capital and go to the countryside. This is where they will experience traditional Bulgarian hospitality firsthand, be stuffed to the gills, shown the new furniture in the sitting room, and be invited for a sleepover, no arguments accepted. In the cities, though, they will witness the following paradox: of all EU capitals, Sofia has the lowest per capita GDP, yet the highest number of expensive Mercedes cars. There is a nonstop competition for who will have the best car, the most expensive villa, and the most fashionable wardrobe in town. Friends and the extended family still matter, but in the cities, personal success becomes more and more important.

RATIONALITY AND EMOTIONALITY

"Generally, Bulgarians are not inclined to succumb to emotional outbursts and revelations of the heart. They rarely disclose their deepest thoughts, secret desires and intentions even to their closest folks. Bulgarians live through their joys and sorrows all alone, and this extremely virtuous restraint reveals a certain suspicion with regard to others as well as a kind of shy chastity, which allows no one entry into the most secret chambers of their hearts. Bulgarians regard intimacy as quite theatrical especially when demonstrated by a foreigner. They become suspicious and then quite convinced that he or she is doing it for a reason."
TODOR PANOV, FATHER OF BULGARIAN SOCIOLOGY

Panov was writing in 1914 about people who had just lived through political, social, and economic turmoil.

A hundred years later we are looking at the products of another turbulent century.

Bulgarians are cool-headed and self-possessed. They rarely react over-excitedly, as they are very self-conscious. This might be the reason they do not yield readily to mob psychology and usually exert self-control in extreme situations. Rationality and pragmatism are highly valued, and the norm.

Emotionally the Bulgarian sense of national identity is an equal mix of pride and shame: a reflection of the complex, contradictory historical fate of the nation, marked by wrong political choices, dramatic losses, long-term dependency on outsiders, and the inability to protect national causes. Bulgarians are probably the strongest critics of everything negative in the country, but they will react heatedly and defensively if a foreigner starts criticizing the same weaknesses. Interestingly, social reactions to the lack of political and economic progress in recent years have become more polarized, emotional, and pronounced.

Initially Bulgarians can give the impression of being too serious, of being reserved and unsmiling—another trait inherited from the times when any foreigner evoked suspicion and mistrust. However, they become very friendly once they get to know the newcomer, to the point of being overly familiar. They are loud, use a lot of body language, and behave just like their Mediterranean "cousins."

RESPECT FOR AGE, STATUS, AND POWER

In traditional cultures like Bulgaria's, respect for age is probably the first family value that children learn. Anyone older than oneself is treated respectfully, and the oldest are accorded the greatest respect. It used to be the norm for a younger person to kiss the hand of the senior family member when returning home. Advice in all matters was sought from the head of the family first and followed to the letter. Younger people would never interrupt when their elders were speaking. The rule "Never speak unless spoken to first" was deeply imbedded in the behavioral patterns of younger people. Nowadays times have changed; nobody kisses hands, and respect has other forms of expression.

The Bulgarian language has many words that explicitly convey respect. *Lelya* (Auntie) and *Chicho* (Uncle) are used by younger people when addressing older non-relatives, such as friends of their parents, or neighbors. If a younger man speaks to an elder, he'll probably add "*Bai*" in front of the name, which shows respect for the older person's age and wisdom. Seniors are also addressed by non-relatives as *Baba* (Granny) or *Dyado* (Grandpa) instead of Madam or Sir, especially in the villages.

Things are pretty different when it comes to social status and political or economic power. History is once again the culprit behind Bulgarians' lack of respect for power in general and politicians in particular. A popular quote from one of the best and brightest Bulgarian classical writers, Aleko Konstantinov, labels all politicians as "*maskara*" (buffoons). Betrayed innumerable times by their political leaders, Bulgarians have little respect for them, and this is still true today; corrupt politicians are a favorite topic of discussion among Bulgarians. Ordinary Bulgarians also have little respect for wealth, and especially for the nouveaux riches, simply because they do not believe anyone can acquire riches so quickly in an honest way. Bulgarians can also often view successful entrepreneurs and business people with envy and jealousy.

MILLENNIALS AND GEN Z: RISING TO THE CHALLENGE

Younger Bulgarians are modern, well-informed, and open to the world. They are mobile, focused, plugged-in, and creative, and are looking for ways that they can improve their quality of life beyond what their parents were able to achieve. They are risk-takers at home and abroad, where many go to study and work. The advantages of democratic choice and freedom of movement, along with easy access to information and new social networks, have given younger Bulgarians opportunities their parents simply never had. And while they may not live, learn, and work in the same financial or cultural environment that their peers from other EU countries do, they face similar problems and share similar goals—to be happy, financially secure, and free.

As throughout much of the West, trends of cohabiting, not having children, and living as a single parent have become more common and socially acceptable in the current decade, particularly among younger generations. While younger Bulgarians today benefit from increased international cooperation and trade as part of the country's integration into the EU, they do face challenges at home. In 2021, the percentage of young people not in education, employment, or training (NEETs) in Bulgaria was above the EU average—18 percent of young Bulgarians (15–29) neither studied nor worked, while 33 percent were engaged in studies and 43 percent worked full-time.

CHAPTER THREE

CUSTOMS & TRADITIONS

PUBLIC HOLIDAYS

The Bulgarian Labor Code regulates all public holidays. In the past, when a public holiday fell on a Tuesday, Wednesday, or Thursday, the Monday or Friday was designated as an official holiday to make a long weekend. In 2016, however, businesses calculated that the bridge holidays incurred 300–400 million leva worth of losses annually and the practice was stopped.

Public holidays in Bulgaria apply to all public institutions including schools, but only schools and universities close on November 1, when the nation celebrates its thinkers and cultural pioneers. Universities have their own celebration on December 8, the day of St. Clement of Ohrid, patron of Sofia State University.

At Christmas, a silver coin is baked into the ritual family bread. Whoever finds the coin will have good luck for the year ahead.

MAJOR RELIGIOUS CELEBRATIONS

Christmas

Christmas is an important religious celebration, and as a country with a wealth of both pagan and Christian traditions, Bulgaria celebrates the birth of Jesus in its own unique way. A lot of rituals, both Christian and pre-Christian, ensure that the coming year will be lucky, plentiful, and joyful. Celebrations start the day before Christmas with Christmas Eve (Budni Vecher) dinner.

The Christmas Eve table serves vegetarian dishes only, and there should be an odd number of them. Ritual bread is a must. There are three types of bread: one for Christmas, the other for the house and farm, and the third for the *koledari* (carol singers named after the holiday, Koleda in Bulgarian), who will be expected

later. The ritual family bread has a silver coin hidden
in it, and after the first piece is broken and dedicated
to the wellbeing of the house, everyone gets a piece,
starting with the eldest. Whoever gets the coin in his or
her piece will have a very lucky year ahead. The table is
not cleared after the meal, so that the souls of the dearly
departed can come and feast during the night.

Then, in the countryside, groups of *koledari*, who are
dressed up, gather and prepare to go on their all-night
rounds. This practice is strictly observed because ancient
belief has it that all the evil forces—devils, vampires, and
ghouls—are now out and about, and only *koledari* songs
can scare them away. The *koledari* start at the houses of
the most important people in the village—the mayor, the
priest, and the teacher. Unlike carol singers in the West,
each member of the *koledari* group has a specific task to
perform besides singing: a "granddad" and a "grandma"
are the comedians, the gift-gatherer collects the food and
money, and there is a *gaida* (bagpipe) player. The group
performs songs wishing long life, good health, love, joy,
and wealth to each person in the family, from the eldest
down to the youngest. The best, though, are dedicated
to the gorgeous maidens whose beauty is brighter than
the sun. An important task of *koledari* is to announce
the rebirth of nature and the establishment of new
order across the universe.

On Christmas Day everybody is back at the table,
where a roast piglet and red wine are waiting for the
merry company of relatives and close friends.

Easter

For Orthodox Christians Easter is the most sacred celebration because the resurrection of Christ is considered the ultimate proof of his divine origin; for believers it is the source of religious fervor. Preparations for the festival continue throughout the previous week. Easter eggs are painted, usually on Thursday or Saturday, but never on Good Friday. Using the first red-painted egg—symbolizing the blood of Christ, life, and victory—grandmothers mark a cross on the foreheads of children to give them health and strength during the year. Red eggs are placed in front of the home icon, laid in the chest of a maiden's dowry, and buried in the fields. On Holy Thursday women start kneading the dough for the Easter breads. These breads are called by different names in different regions of Bulgaria: Easter buns, Lord's bread, egg bread, "twist," or "doll." Usually, Easter breads are decorated with an odd number of red or white eggs with dough twisted around them. Women also prepare smaller Easter buns with one red egg in the middle: they are given to the first guest, to the husband's brother, and the wife's brother.

Easter is celebrated for three days. The Orthodox Easter service begins two hours before midnight on the Saturday night. Worshipers carry a red-painted egg, and when the priest announces the resurrection of Christ there is general rejoicing; the congregants eat their eggs, so ending the Easter fast. Everybody leaves the church with a burning candle, carrying it carefully so that it arrives home still alight.

Sunday, Monday, and Tuesday are given over to joyous celebrations. Traditionally, people get together to dance in the square. At this time parents are carefully watching and picking out future spouses for their sons and daughters. Everybody is wearing new clothes, especially the girls, to show that they are hardworking and have made their own dresses. This is a time to visit relatives, and, wherever one goes, a richly laid table is awaiting. People greet each other with the phrase "*Christos vozkrese*" ("Christ is risen"), and the reply is "*Voistina vozkrese*" ("Indeed, he is risen").

May 6: St. George's Day

This is one of the greatest Bulgarian Orthodox holidays, recognized by all: believers celebrate the patron saint of farmers, and non-believers celebrate the name day (George is the most popular name for Bulgarian males) and the day of the Bulgarian Army, dedicated to its soldiers' courage and resilience, as St. George is its patron saint.

A Bulgarian folk song says, "Easter is great, but St. George's Day is greater." The day marks the approach of summer and the active farming season. Bulgarians believe that the year will be bountiful if it rains on St. George's Day. "Each raindrop on St. George's Day will bring a gold coin into the purse," the saying goes. For this reason many rituals are performed on this day, the most important of which is the slaughter of a sacrificial lamb—always the first-born male animal. Early in the morning it is adorned with a garland of flowers and herbs, and a candle is attached to its horns. Then it is ceremoniously fed with fresh grass and given salt to lick—the tradition being that there will then be ample food for all the other animals throughout the coming year.

Another tradition is to take the red Easter egg to the fields and bury it there, so that the harvest will be rich and plentiful. The family member who gets up first goes to the meadows to pick nettles, and then brushes everybody's bare feet with them so that evil will not be able to catch up with them all year long. A special ritual, oval bread (pita) is prepared and decorated with figurines of sheep, shepherds, and wheat sheaves.

St. George's Day is a big community holiday. Large groups of people gather together to eat, dance, and have fun. When the roast lambs have been eaten their bones are buried in the ground. These are celebrations you can still witness in the Bulgarian countryside. City-dwellers buy their lamb and try to follow the traditions as best as they can. There is a military parade in every large city with a garrison, and orchestras perform on the squares where people dance the traditional *horo* and *rachenitza*.

IMPORTANT CIVIC CELEBRATIONS

New Year

While Christmas is a family-oriented holiday, the New Year is the perfect time to get together with friends and go to open-air concerts, firework displays, and wild parties around town. Shortly before midnight, the president of Bulgaria delivers his New Year address to the nation, then the countdown starts, and at midnight the national anthem is played and everybody sings along. You will see tears here and there—Bulgarians are an emotional and patriotic lot. There is a lot of drinking, dancing, and singing into the early hours of the first day of the New Year, but then it's St. Basil's Day, followed by St. John's and St. Jordan's Day, and ten more name days; January is truly a month of celebrations, parties, and visits to friends and relatives. A tradition that comes with the New Year is *surovakane*: small children with beautifully decorated dogwood or willow switches go around and ritually "whip" elder relatives and even strangers on their backs, wishing them luck, health, and wealth in exchange for some money or sweet treats.

March 3: Liberation Day

This is a solemn celebration, much like Remembrance Day in Great Britain and Canada. On this day Bulgarians revere the memory of the great patriotic endeavors of tens of thousands of heroes who fought

Folk dancers perform at the Center for Culture and Education, Atrium, in Nesebar on Liberation Day, March 3.

and lost their lives for the freedom and independence of Bulgaria. Special liturgies at the cathedrals in the largest cities and ceremonies in the city squares mark the beginning of the celebrations. The grand liturgy at the St. Alexander Nevski Cathedral in the capital is performed by the head of the Bulgarian Orthodox Church, the Patriarch himself, and is attended by politicians, public figures, and prominent citizens. Many Bulgarians bring flowers to the monuments of the fallen to remember and commemorate their courage and self-sacrifice. Orchestras and troupes perform lively music and folk dances for the public.

May 24: Saints Cyril and Methodius Day

This day is also known as Alphabet, Culture, and Education Day. Saint Cyril and Saint Methodius are the most celebrated saints in the Orthodox Church, and not only that—in 1980 Pope John Paul II declared the two brothers co-patron saints of Europe. Icons of them can be found in every Bulgarian church. Russia, the Former Republic of Macedonia, the Czech Republic, and Slovakia all celebrate the brothers who created the Slavonic alphabet in the ninth century. In Bulgaria, students of all ages bring flowers and green branches, and weave wreaths to decorate the entrance gates of their schools. The first celebration, on May 24, 1851, was in Plovdiv's Saints Cyril and Methodius High School. Today students participate in processions, concerts, exhibitions, and various cultural events, while high school seniors get ready for their graduation parties. It is the most exciting day of the year for students all over the country.

NAME DAYS

Unlike the Catholic tradition of ascribing a saint's name to each day of the year, name days in Bulgaria are days associated not only with Eastern Orthodox saints but with biblical events. There are more than 130 name days throughout the year. Some of these days are great religious holidays, such as St. George's Day and Virgin Mary Day (Bogoroditza). On other days, like the Day of Theodore (Todorovden), there are horse races related to the legend of the fourth-century St. Theodore, who rode a white horse and went to God to ask him to send summer to Earth—so this holiday is also known as Horse Easter. Todorovden is also dedicated to newlywed brides; rituals for health and fertility are performed, and the young women bake bread for approval by their in-laws. In another tradition newlywed women prepare a batch of small loaves and give them to friends and relatives, and receive wishes to have many children in the future.

Jordan's Day (Yordanovden) is associated not with a saint but with an important Christian event: Jesus' baptism in the River Jordan. On this day Orthodox

Each year on January 6, Bulgarian men celebrate Epiphany by dancing in the freezing waters of the Tundzha river in the town of Kalofer.

priests throw a metal cross into a river, the sea, or a lake, and young men jump in to retrieve it. Custom has it that whoever brings it out will be healthy and lucky throughout the year.

Traditionally, guests don't need an invitation to attend a name day party: those who celebrate must be prepared to serve food and drink to anyone who honors them by stopping by to visit and offer their best wishes. Many name days are associated with specific foods. For example, on St. Nicolas Day, the day of the patron saint of sailors and fishermen, fish is the traditional food on the table.

Name days are often celebrated in a more elaborate and stylish way, with many more guests, gifts, and best wishes than birthdays. The attention Bulgarians pay to marking and celebrating name days shows the importance of one's name and the honor attached to it. Though younger people may prefer to get together in a bar or a restaurant, the food, music, and celebration will be marked by the traditions associated with the patron saint of the day.

NATURE AND FOLK FESTIVALS

Bulgarians have a high time on many other occasions, not just public holidays. They celebrate nature and its gifts, their love for dance and music, and, above all, their spirit of togetherness. In some ways the country is a kaleidoscope of live performances and events all year round. If you are lucky enough to be in the countryside at the right time, you'll see villagers in folk costumes celebrating an ancient festival just as their forebears did—the same music, the same dances, the same colorful attire on young and old alike. It's enough to hear the first few notes of the popular *horo* to want to join the line and start hopping and skipping in step with everyone else; not a single celebration goes without music and dancing.

Around March 1, you will notice twisted red and white woolen thread adornments on people's lapels or wrists—the *marteniza*. The wearing of this magical amulet is an ancient pagan tradition marking the coming of spring. The name comes from a character in Balkan folklore, a lame old woman called Baba (Grandma) Marta, who carries an iron walking stick. She is notoriously capricious and unstable. When she smiles, the sun shines; when she's angry, cold weather grips the earth. Most of the rituals associated with Baba Marta are aimed at appeasing her. The occasion also brings wishes for health and fertility at the beginning of the new cycle in nature. People smile because they trust that by wearing *marteniza* on the first of March they have won the benevolence of Baba Marta and that it will bring them health, wealth, and happiness.

Bulgaria is the country of roses; it is the number one exporter of rose oil and other rose products, and

Young women dressed in traditional clothing celebrate the annual Rose Festival.

there is a festival dedicated to this beautiful and quite lucrative flower. The Balkan town of Troyan celebrates the plum, a humble fruit used to make the famous Bulgarian plum brandy (*slivova rakia*).

Another very special day is Trifon Zarezan, the celebration of winemaking, winemakers, and the patron of vineyards, St. Trifon. Wine has been produced in the Bulgarian lands for thousands of years, and is a great source of pride.

Bulgarian folk music is celebrated widely. Three of the best-known festivals are the International Folk Festival in Koprivshtiza, the "Pirin Sings" festival of Bulgarian and Macedonian folk music, and the Rozhen Sabor, an open-air festival of Rhodopean music. These festivals attract hundreds of visitors from around the country and abroad.

Bulgarians wear traditional costumes to celebrate Kukeri on January 14.

Every Bulgarian city has its own regional festival, where amateur troupes demonstrate their skills and love of all music and dance Bulgarian.

WEDDINGS, BIRTHS, CHOOSING NAMES

Bulgarians typically marry by individual choice, although families may exert pressure. Arranged marriages are common among some groups, such as Muslims and Roma, though less so today than they once were. Only civil ceremonies are legally recognized, but many couples will also have a religious ceremony. In Bulgaria today, women and men generally marry in their late twenties and early thirties respectively, whereas in the past both would have been likely to marry in their mid-twenties. It is still most common for spouses to be from the same ethnic and religious background. Because it was

Traditionally, weddings must be witnessed by another married couple, known as the *kumove*.

considered dishonorable, divorce in the past was rare, but has become far more common; today almost half of all marriages end in divorce. Marriage rates declined in the 1990s in response to the uncertainty of the times, and in 2011 Bulgaria reported the lowest marriage rate among EU countries: 2.9 per 1,000 inhabitants. By 2021 this figure had recovered somewhat and rose to 3.9 marriages per 1,000 inhabitants.

Traditionally, weddings are the merriest and most cherished celebrations because they mark the beginning of a new family, future children, and accumulation of wealth for the clan. In the past, the rituals were elaborate, and the preparation took some time. Today only a few of the must-do wedding rituals are performed; for example, the sweet bread (*blaga pita*) that the mother of the bridegroom feeds the newlyweds upon their entry into the reception hall or restaurant where the wedding guests are entertained by a wedding singer and orchestra.

There is no best man, maid of honor, or bridesmaids and friends of the groom. Instead, a married couple—this is still a must—witnesses the act of marriage and signs the marriage papers together with the newlyweds. This couple is called *kumove* (witnesses) and is considered part of the extended family from that day on. These two will also be godparents to the children born to the new couple. They play a very important role in the organization of the wedding party—very much like the best man and maid of honor—and are expected to make a substantial gift to the new family.

The giving of wedding gifts is also different. The couple does not request anything specific. It's usual to give cash in an envelope rather than, say, a crystal bowl or a check. In the villages, to show off their generosity, guests pin money to the bride's dress so that she starts looking like a multicolored bird with banknotes for feathers—a custom considered vulgar by city dwellers.

Children are expected to follow reasonably soon after. Although modern times have influenced attitudes, many still hope that the first-born will be a son. A baby son will most likely be named after his paternal grandfather, to continue the tradition of the name and honor the eldest member of the clan. If a girl is born, the name of the grandfather gets a suffix to change the gender. For example, Ivan becomes Ivanka or Vanya, and George turns into Gergana. Light blue and pink are the colors associated with a baby boy and a baby girl, and there are numerous customs related to pregnancy and birth.

FUNERALS

It is not customary to announce a death in the newspaper; this is a relatively new phenomenon. Instead, a brief eulogy—and sometimes a solemn poem—with a picture of the deceased is printed on a flyer called a *necrolog* (obituary) and stuck on buildings, lamp posts, and the front door of the house of the bereaved. Another printed obituary is circulated on the fortieth day of passing, and then on the third month, ninth month, and each year afterward. Close family members wear black for a year, while village widows never stop wearing black. In villages, it's the church bell that announces a death. People learn of the passing by word of mouth, and gather in the house of the deceased, where a room is prepared for the all-night, open-coffin wake. Emotions are high, and mourning is open and demonstrative. In the past, one or more women were invited and paid to wail and cry bitterly behind the coffin on the way to the cemetery to show how much the dearly departed was missed. Bulgarian funerals are dramatic, and sometimes suprisingly so for outsiders coming from more restrained cultures.

SOME SUPERSTITIONS

Bulgarian culture abounds in superstitions of all sorts. Throwing salt behind your back, or "spitting" twice are trusted methods of warding off evil. Weddings, pregnancy, and death have the greatest number of superstitions.

Weddings and Marriage

- The longer the wedding dress, the longer and happier the marriage will be.
- The wedding dress shouldn't be backless, otherwise adultery will ruin the marriage.
- The bride should always have a red thread on her to ward off the evil eye, and she should never wear pearls—they symbolize tears.
- The dress should not be taken to the cleaners before the first baby is born.
- A popular custom associated with Bulgarian marriage is the "stepping on the foot" immediately after the ceremony: the one who steps on the foot of his or her spouse first will "wear the pants" in their future family life.
- To drop your wedding ring is very bad luck.
- Once she has left her parents' home, the bride should not return there for at least three days.

Pregnancy and Birth

- The young wife should keep her pregnancy a secret for the first trimester so as not to bring misfortune and premature death to the baby. She must announce it immediately after the trimester; if she delays the news the baby will have speech problems later.

- There is no baby shower for a Bulgarian baby—it's considered very bad luck to buy anything for an unborn child, in case of stillbirth.
- Mother and baby don't leave the house for the first forty days for many different reasons, but mostly to ward off the evil eye and protect the newborn.

Death
- During the all-night wake no one should fall asleep. A close vigil is kept as many people believe that the dead will turn into a vampire if an animal should jump over the corpse.
- All mirrors in the house should be covered for forty days so that the soul of the departed doesn't return.
- Never jump over an empty grave, because one who does will die soon.
- A grave should not be left empty overnight.
- When bringing flowers to a funeral, their number should always be even. On any other occasion, flowers should come in odd numbers. Chrysanthemums are considered flowers of death and should never be given on any other occasion.
- Returning from the cemetery, one should not turn back lest another person die soon.
- The mourners should not continue weeping, as the deceased will feel confused and be drawn back to Earth.
- If a butterfly appears while relatives are visiting a grave, it is the dead person's soul: to catch it would trap their soul.

CHAPTER FOUR

MAKING FRIENDS

FRIENDSHIP FOR BULGARIANS

Like most collectivist cultures, Bulgarian society places great importance on personal relationships. Friendships start very early and generally continue throughout life. Forged in the neighborhood, at school, university, and then the workplace, friendships are invaluable and irreplaceable. The friend of a family member automatically becomes a friend of the family. This is how Bulgarians develop their social networks. Adult Bulgarians will find statements such as "making new friends is a part of personal growth" hard to understand. Unlike people from individualist cultures, where friends come and go with the tides of life, Bulgarians feel loyal to their families first and to their friends next, generally placing allegiance to an employer or authority far below on their priorities list. After all, having

Bulgarians value their friendships, often making friends for life from a young age. Here, old friends sit together in Ruse.

friends—and not just in high places—solves most of the problems one faces in everyday life.

Despite Todor Panov's 1914 portrait of shyness and reserve as the deep "invisible" layers of the Bulgarian soul (see page 79), on the "visible" level, the observable ways in which Bulgarians communicate with close friends appear to be both extravert and intrusive.

Many foreigners will find the intimacy of the relationship among Bulgarian friends almost unbearable, as it leaves no privacy whatsoever. As we have seen, there is no word for "privacy" in the Bulgarian language. This is one possible reason that foreigners might feel isolated in the company of Bulgarians; they feel frustrated by the ostensible harshness, the openness, the honesty—too much of it at times—and the full range of emotional, intellectual, financial, political, and philosophical matters that are thrown into the conversation— the ingredients of a true, strong friendship most Bulgarians share.

As for social acquaintances, any foreigner who truly wants to get to know Bulgaria will find it easy to strike up an acquaintanceship with a local person speaking at least one of the European languages. Recent numbers show that 70 percent of young Bulgarians speak good English. Their language skills usually come either from graduating from a language high school (elite schools established many years ago) or having studied at university abroad, or simply from a love of Western pop culture. Without the language barrier, a visitor to Bulgaria can quite quickly get into the whirlwind of social life. To build a real friendship will take time, though. As Bulgarians like to say, to become real friends, two people must eat a bag of salt together first (that is, spend a lot of time together). The best way for outsiders to break into the intimate circle of Bulgarian friends will be to make an effort and start learning the language. It will be highly appreciated.

MEETING PEOPLE

In the words of two American expats in Sofia, it's really hard to "put your foot in the door" when it comes to making friends with Bulgarians and growing fledgling friendships in a country where one doesn't know the language or the culture. It's also not so easy to learn what Bulgarians' likes and dislikes are and how they like to spend their spare time. This is a pretty normal reaction. In countries like Bulgaria expats tend to frequent a number of bars and restaurants where locals rarely go. There are two reasons for this. The first is that Bulgarians prefer to visit their friends, enjoy delicious homemade food, have as much to drink as they like, listen to their preferred music, and carry on their own conversations in a familiar atmosphere. The second reason is that not many locals can afford to go out on a regular basis. This doesn't mean they don't get together and have a great time—they just do it at home with their friends. On the other hand, for most working expats, going out to a familiar bar "where everybody knows your name" is the easy option for having a good time at the end of the week.

However, just like everywhere else, friendship is forged by shared interests and shared experiences. No doubt the workplace will be the first place to meet people once you are in Bulgaria. If you are reluctant to lose your privacy and want to keep things professional at work, then finding activities you enjoy and doing them in the company of people who share your love for them is another great way to start looking for friends. This could be the gym, dance classes, hiking, football—go wherever your interests are to meet like-minded people. Once you've found what you like to do and a group of people to do it with, then you'll probably receive an invitation to join the group for dinner or a drink, and you'll have made at least a dozen new acquaintances. If you are a woman in Sofia, the International Women's Club is a great place for making friends. They have monthly meetings and events to help ease your transition to living in Bulgaria and can be found at www.iwc-sofia.com.

Expat organizations (such as www.internations. org) have monthly meetings and events to help ease your transition to living in Bulgaria. You just need to be open and willing to make the effort. If you would like to meet up with someone you want to make friends with, get their number and call them to do something—this could be the beginning of a beautiful friendship! In short, there aren't too many obstacles to making new friends in Bulgaria apart from self-imposed ones, so make that call. You could also offer to teach your native language in exchange for Bulgarian lessons, and may make a good friend this way, too.

FAVORS AND THE RIGHT CONNECTIONS

In Bulgaria, relatives by blood and marriage on both the husband and the wife's sides are considered family or clan. Rather than formal structures, clans are broad informal networks of relatives. Add all friends and neighbors into the mix, and you are looking at *blizki*, or "the close" people. More distant relatives may interact less frequently because they probably don't live in the same town. Rapid urbanization during socialist times scattered people all over the country; the older family members stayed back in the villages and small towns while the young generations left to work in the factories or go to college and find a good job in the cities. However, it is not uncommon to find clusters of close relatives in rural communities even to this day, especially among Roma and Muslim communities. Connections through rural and urban networks of *blizki* were often mobilized to accomplish such objectives as obtaining scarce goods, accessing information, getting into a good school, or gaining employment. The phrase "to have the right guy for the job" means that one knows someone who can arrange for the accomplishment of the task at hand. Such favors are rarely paid for but are returned when the time comes.

The term "connections" used to have negative connotations because it presupposed a substitution of skills, education, and experience with being a relative or friend of the decision-making personnel manager. However, with growing Western influence this concept has recently acquired more positive connotations—connections are also established thanks to one's own abilities, from high school to university and throughout the course of an entire career, and one's professional network has been built through one's own contacts, achievements, and interests. No one would think a person used "connections" if they did really well at university and were invited to stay on after graduation, or were recommended to a prospective employer by their professor. The winds of change have started to blow away the old perceptions of how things get done in Bulgaria.

SOCIALIZING

There are a few points to be made about Bulgarians and socializing. Unlike North Americans, Bulgarians really mean it when they ask you how you are, or how you feel. They expect an honest answer (not the ubiquitous "Great!" that you hear in the US or Canada), and will listen to your good news and bad news carefully, trying to figure out a way to help or simply sympathize with you. In a word, "How are you?" should be taken literally. Naturally, when asked about their situation, they will offer a detailed, and

Friends gather to share drinks in Sofia.

often personal answer; after all, why did you ask if you were not truly interested?

Bulgarians may not be as punctual as their Western acquaintances or colleagues, but they will spend a lot more of their personal time getting to know you better, trying to be helpful, offering their local know-how and connections to get things done. Bulgarians will scrap their weekend plans to take a visiting foreign colleague to a place of beauty and reverence, such as the Rila Monastery, southwest of Sofia, or out to lunch. In a nutshell, their time will be yours as long as you need advice or company.

INVITATIONS HOME

Once you have become closer acquaintances, you will definitely receive an invitation to visit them. Bulgarian hospitality and generosity are fabled because Bulgarians like to impress and pamper their guests. You will most probably be invited to a birthday party, or a name day party (although Bulgarians know there is no need for invitations on that day—anyone is welcome to join in the party), or it will be a party dedicated to you, the guest of honor.

Whatever the occasion, expect a lot of food. Bulgarians love aperitifs, so there'll be drinks and salads, dips and snacks of all sorts before the main course arrives. Very often a guest has eaten his fill before the main meal of the evening arrives on the table. Keep this in mind, and go easy on the appetizers. The host will serve drinks all night long, so if you want no more, leave your glass half full.

The meal will certainly be meat, so, if you are a vegetarian or vegan, it is a good idea to say so in advance, so as not to disappoint or embarrass your hosts. The food will be served in large bowls with serving utensils, so everyone helps themselves to as much as they want on to their own plate, and you can ask what's in the bowl if it looks unfamiliar. If you can't eat more, just leave what you can't manage on your plate. They will then want you to do justice to the dessert, but if you explain that you only take an espresso after such a great meal, everyone will understand—many Bulgarians decline dessert in favor of coffee. It isn't considered rude to decline food or drink if you offer a plausible explanation. Yet, if traditional homemade desserts are served— for example, *dobush torte* (a buttercream layer cake)—it wouldn't be wise to decline, as they really are delicious.

GIFT GIVING

No matter what the occasion, you should always bring a gift. When Bulgarians go to a party, they bring a bottle of wine or any drink they know will appeal to the host's taste. The more thoughtful will also bring flowers for the hostess and chocolate for the children, if any. The flowers should be an odd number—even numbers are brought to funerals only. If the occasion is a birthday or a name day party, gifts should be chosen accordingly.

The following three "golden rules" will always make the host happy. First, take a personal gift—not something that will be used by the whole family. Second, the price tag is not as important as the thought and the attention you pay in choosing the right gift. Finally, don't go for very expensive gifts. Bulgarians will try to reciprocate even if they can't afford it. The best choice is a souvenir or food or drink typical of your country, which will spark off a lengthy discussion about food, drink, and different tastes around the world.

There are a couple of objects that don't make good gifts and should be avoided at all costs. Don't give knives as a gift, no matter how rare or original they are. Another no-no is a handkerchief: it symbolizes departure, and is never given as a present, no matter how pretty it is.

DATING

Many male visitors to Bulgaria assert that the highest number of beautiful women per square meter can be found in the streets of Sofia. The first thing that most people notice about Bulgarian women is their amazingly dark, shiny hair. In Mediterranean countries most women have the expected combination of olive skin and either dark brown or black hair and brown eyes; in Bulgaria, many women are light skinned but have jet-black hair and hazel, green, or blue eyes—a fascinating combination pointing to a mix of genes.

Certain chat-up lines will fall flat. The Western visitor may be tempted to employ familiar strategies: either approaching women directly on the street or in the coffee shop, or seizing any opportunity that presents itself. Here is what he will probably learn very fast. First, if you see a confident, well-dressed woman, chances are that she will already have a serious boyfriend, if not a husband. Second, telling girls that you are an American from New York will elicit a lukewarm response. Thanks to the numerous movies and TV shows allowing anyone to live there vicariously, practically everyone has already "been to New York." A Western friend experimented by telling girls he was a Russian from Moscow, and he received slightly more interested reactions. A girl who has studied abroad, or is still a student there, would be much friendlier toward American or Western men, but this doesn't mean much. Remember, Bulgarians are good at being hospitable, but their hospitality shouldn't be mistaken for personal interest.

Bulgarians would rather date someone they have known previously from their neighborhood, school, university, or work than a stranger whom they've just met. They feel much more comfortable with someone who shares their sense of the world, interests, friends, and cultural heritage. Things like blind dates or speed dating seem quite alien to Bulgarians—they are neither popular nor commonly practiced. Foreigners will be readily approached if in obvious need of assistance, but not for escapades of any sort or flirting for the sake of flirting. Emotional relationships are taken seriously, and always a step at a time. Playful behavior or laughing at someone's jokes is not a sign of sexual interest, but simply a demonstration of goodwill and enjoyment of pleasant company.

Bulgarians are highly tolerant of physical proximity; you will see people hugging and kissing or fixing their friend's tie or collar—this is not a sign of emotional involvement, just the degree to which they are close friends and feel comfortable with each other.

As in most of Eastern Europe, smiling and eye contact directed at strangers is generally a sign of weakness. Southern European men, who tend to look much like Bulgarians, will probably receive almost no eye contact in Bulgaria: relying on eye contact as an indicator of interest is not a good idea, and one will have to work to get noticed. The Balkans is one of the most conservative regions in Europe when it comes to dating and courtship. Don't expect to fly into Sofia for a weekend and start dating right away.

Things have changed somewhat since the introduction of dating apps and Web sites, though, both of which have become more popular in recent years, particularly since the coronavirus pandemic forced people indoors. The Serious Relationships Web site (www.serioznizapoznanstva.com) is advertised as a no-fake profiles site, while www.zapoznalnik. com is free and boasts more than seventy thousand members. Internationally popular apps like Hinge and Tinder are popular among younger Bulgarians, especially those who speak a second language.

CHAPTER FIVE

AT HOME

FAMILY LIFE

In Bulgaria today you will still find at least two generations living under the same roof, even if only on a seasonal basis. People often bring their aged parents to their own apartment in the city during the cold season to save on the heating bills and help with daily chores such as grocery shopping and cooking. In turn, the elderly take care of their grandchildren during the day and babysit. This way, a very strong bond develops between children and their grandparents. Single people rarely live on their own if their parents are still alive. It is the norm to live in the parental home and take care of your mother and father if you have no children of your own. Families have breakfast and dinner together, and it is considered impolite to leave the table before the oldest family member has finished eating.

Many Bulgarians have a city dwelling and a weekend home in the country, where summers are spent.

The connection with the land is still very strong, and Bulgarians use every opportunity to leave the city and go to their "villa" (generally a modest house) in the countryside. There, the older family members usually take up gardening and grow their own vegetables, which they then turn into preserves for the winter. It's not only economy and a matter of personal pride; it's also having organic, or "ecologically clean" food, as Bulgarians call it, on their table almost all year round.

HOUSING

Bulgarians tend to be very proud of their traditional urban architecture, which is the result of a complex web of cross-cultural influences. These nineteenth-century high-bourgeois buildings reflect a strong influence of European and Ottoman Baroque designs, yet the mixing of Ottoman and European elements is regarded as typical of the Bulgarian Revival style, examples of which can be seen in the old parts of many Bulgarian towns. Today, though, the majority of city dwellers live in tall, gray, Soviet-era apartment buildings with multiple entrances; small, graffiti-covered elevator cabins—unsuitable for the claustrophobic—take you to the upper floors.

While in the West this type of high-rise building is usually associated with the less well-educated, blue-collar stratum of society, it never had this reputation in post-war socialist Bulgarian cities. All people were meant to

Traditional homes in Plovdiv's Old Town.

be equal, so doctors, writers, and teachers lived side by side with factory workers, plumbers, and streetcar drivers. Between some of these buildings there are still tree-lined playgrounds where retirees like to sit and socialize, gossiping and discussing topics of the day while their grandchildren run around and play on the swings. Most occupants own their flats. There are no underground parking lots, so cars are parked in the streets around the buildings, but each apartment has its own basement storage room.

Things started to change in the 1990s. Modern apartment blocks with 24/7 security and modern amenities were constructed, becoming very popular with those who could not afford their own detached house. People with more money started moving out to private suburban villas. Still, in cities like Sofia and Plovdiv, most people continue to live in concrete high-rises.

INSIDE THE BULGARIAN HOME

The construction boom in Bulgaria has resulted in many new houses in the suburbs and apartment buildings in the cities, comparable to the kind of housing one finds in Europe and North America. Many gated communities have pools, gyms, and even convenience stores, but you will only see those in the three biggest cities in the country.

A young family at home.

The apartments in the oldest high-rise buildings don't boast fancy design, but do have central heating and running water, together with all the necessary appliances of a contemporary household, although many are still furnished with furniture from the 1970s and 1980s. Homes and their interior design and décor, however, reflect the personal tastes and preferences of the owners as well as the size of their family. No matter how old the furniture is, the woman of the house makes it her daily chore to keep it clean and shining. There is a lot on display in the sitting room, including Bulgarian treasures or souvenirs from abroad. Embroidery and needlework are popular forms of decoration, and you will see flowers everywhere—Bulgarian women are famous for their green thumbs. Bookcases and bookshelves have an honorable place in the home, showing both the literary tastes of the hosts and how well-read they are.

The kitchen is the heart and soul of the home: apartments have kitchens large enough to accommodate a table where the family can gather for meals. When guests come to visit, they are usually invited to the sitting room, where there is another dining table, typically expandable, for more formal dinners. The TV is also in the sitting room. TVs are not commonly found in bedrooms, because Bulgarians like to watch television together, comment on the show, and argue with the TV presenter if they feel like it.

Most detached houses have a so-called summer kitchen—a semi-covered open space at garden level where meals are prepared when the weather is hot. Older houses even have their own old-style ovens for making homemade bread and roast lamb or pork on holidays such as Christmas and Easter.

THE DAILY ROUND

For many working Bulgarians and their school-age children the day begins early. Breakfast tends to be a quick slice of bread and cheese and a cup of coffee. Primary and secondary schools run their classes in two shifts, so the morning shift begins at 7:30 a.m. for students in Grades 5 to 11, and at 8:20 a.m. for younger students in Grades 1 to 4. Buses in the large cities and Sofia's street cars run from 5:00 a.m. until midnight: there are no school buses, so children either take the regular city transportation or their parents or grandparents drive them to school.

Government office hours are from 9:00 a.m. to 5:30 p.m., while banks are open from 9:00 a.m. to 4:30 p.m., but despite a well-developed city transportation system many people prefer to drive to work, and morning and evening rush hours on the road can be extremely frustrating. As working women usually do the shopping after leaving the office, large supermarkets such as Carrefour are open until 9:30 p.m. Smaller retailers such as neighborhood convenience stores may be open until much later.

Bulgarians took enthusiastically to the arrival of the supermarket chains. The introduction of electronic methods of payment is another reason why more than 55 percent shop at hypermarkets. These attract more and more customers with regular promotions and quite a few people—usually frugal retirees—go shopping only during promotion times.

Fruit and vegetables are usually bought at the local vegetable markets: all large cities have an open-air market in summer and fall, and covered stalls in the colder months. Stalls offer seasonal fruit and vegetables grown locally as well as imported from nearby countries like Turkey and Greece. Locally grown or locally produced delicacies like tomatoes, potatoes, various nuts, honey, fruit preserves, pickles,

A couple buys vegetables from a market in Sofia.

dried fruit, herbs, and spices are always bought at the city marketplaces.

On weekdays most Bulgarians enjoy a quiet family dinner at home, and, after the TV news, a reality show or a Turkish soap opera, which have long been popular in Bulgaria. Most people go to bed at about 11:00 p.m. On weekends they typically leave the cities, go visiting, or hang out with friends.

THE COST OF LIVING

Living in Bulgaria is much cheaper than in any other EU country. Rental prices are very reasonable. For example, in 2022 the apartment rental price per square meter in Sofia was between 4 and 10 euros, depending on location, size, and whether or not the place was furnished. Houses could be rented as cheaply as 450 euros, rising to 6,000 euros in the city center. It is much cheaper to rent in the provincial cities. Apart from hotels and cheap hostels, visitors on a budget can also stay at Airbnb apartments which are available in all major Bulgarian cities. For example, in 2022 an apartment in Sofia city center could be found for below 50 euros per night.

Public transportation is also very cheap. Passengers can buy single tickets, pre-paid cards, or monthly, bimonthly, and annual passes. A single Sofia city transport ticket costs 85 eurocents, but it's cheaper to get a metro e-card for 6 euros that is good for 10 journeys in a day. A metro e-card can be purchased from station ticket counters and more money can be added to the card. When traveling by bus, trolleybuses, tram, or the metro, you can use your contactless credit or debit card, or you can buy a ticket from the bus or tram driver with cash. Going by train is the cheapest option for traveling around: a distance of around 30 miles (50 km) will cost up to 2 euros. A bus fare is 1 euro on top of the train fare. Taxis are cheaper than anywhere in Europe, but some taxi drivers tend to overcharge foreigners. For more on hailing cabs, see page 156.

Food is inexpensive, too, unless it's imported from the other side of the world and is out of season. A doctor's visit is anywhere between 7 and 25 euros. Secondary education is free. While universities charge fees, they are very low for EU citizens compared to those charged by North American universities. Electric energy costs 7 cents per KW, diesel and gas are approximately 1.5 euros per liter, though these are rising. Dinner for two with good wine may come to 45 euros, but in most places you can find a nice meal for 10 to 15 euros. Beer is very cheap, as is coffee: you can buy a large plastic 2-liter bottle of local beer for 1.5 euros. Movie tickets cost between 4 and 6 euros. The Covid-19 pandemic, supply chain issues, and increasing energy costs are all currently contributing to rising inflation in Bulgaria, and so you may find that certain costs have increased by the time you arrive.

TWENTY-FIRST-CENTURY EDUCATION

Education is state funded through the Ministry of Education and Science and is compulsory for children from seven to sixteen years of age. The Bulgarian educational system follows the continental European tradition.

Basic education covers primary school (Grades 1 to 4) and junior high school (Grades 5 to 8). High school takes either four or five years and is provided in three types of school: comprehensive (general) secondary schools; "profile-oriented," which are specialized skills-based schools, including foreign-language schools; and vocational technical schools. The curriculum is unified for all schools. The school year is divided into two terms: the first starts on September 15 and ends at the end of January, and the second runs from February to the end of June. At the end of each term students receive grades in each subject, and at the end of the school year they get final grades in the subjects. Upon graduation students receive a Diploma of Secondary Education or Secondary Specialized Education.

Private schools are also being established and are beginning to compete successfully with state schools. With the exception of foreign and the specialized foreign-language schools, the official language of instruction is Bulgarian. Ethnic minority children can study their mother tongue within the general

St. Kliment Ohridski, Sofia University.

curriculum. In specialized language schools and in
the profile-oriented schools, instruction takes place
in English, German, Italian, French, Spanish, Turkish,
Armenian, Hebrew, Russian, and other languages.
At university level, instruction takes place in English
at the American University in Bulgaria, and in
German, French, and English in some programs
in the polytechnic universities.

Admission to the thirty-seven public and fourteen
private higher-education institutions in Bulgaria differs
from most European and North American countries

as it is based on the results of written entry exams.
Depending on their desired university and specialty,
candidates write one or more competitive exams or
school-specific tests, and then must submit a diploma
of completed secondary education. The autonomy of
the higher education institutions allows them to set
their own requirements for enrolment every year. This
enables them to organize admission in some specialties
on the basis of a diploma of secondary education
only, or a combination of a diploma with a test or
exams. The application procedure for each specialty is
determined on an annual basis and is made public in
the institution's prospectus.

The number of international students in the
Bulgarian higher education institutions is growing
steadily. In 2020–21, 17,000 students from Greece,
Great Britain, Germany, Ukraine, North Macedonia,
and other countries studied in Bulgaria, the majority
of whom studied in medical universities (62.1 percent).

EMPLOYMENT

Bulgaria is one of the poorest countries in the EU, yet
unemployment figures—just over 4 percent in April
2022—show that it is doing better than other southern
European countries such as Greece, Spain, and
Portugal. The country has been trying to convince its
young talent not to leave and to attract some of its well-

educated emigrants to return with events such as the annual job fair called "Career in Bulgaria. Why Not?" After eleven successful years, the job fair transitioned online at www.careershow.bg. Foreigners come to these events, too, and they are more welcome in Bulgaria than in many Western European countries. In early 2022, Prime Minister Petkov even went so far as to propose paying full scholarships for talented students to study abroad and then return to Bulgaria to work. The country needs so much in terms of development that it is a great place for enthusiastic young people who love to try new things and who want to get good hands-on experience. Most educated younger Bulgarians speak English so there is little in the way of a language barrier. Sofia may not be as fast as London or as fashionable as Milan, but speed and fashion are well compensated for by a pleasant climate, friendly locals, beautiful natural surroundings, and a low cost of living.

CHAPTER SIX

TIME OUT

Bulgarians work for 220 to 230 days and enjoy 135 to 145 days of weekends, holidays, and vacation days in a calendar year. Four out of five employees take their twenty-day vacation in the summer months. Long winter vacations are not popular: skiing weekends are the norm. The most popular way to spend your vacation is the "villacation" at the countryside villa (cottage). Going to the Black Sea is the second most popular, although mountain-trekking and traveling to national places of interest is becoming more widespread. Many Bulgarians like to vacation in Turkey and Greece, while the wealthier travel to more exotic countries, such as Thailand or Bali. Those with the means to do so will also go on short trips for Christmas or Easter—London, Rome, Vienna, and Berlin are the preferred destinations. Younger people enjoy holidaying in groups, while their parents are more likely to spend their holidays on their own, or in the company of a close circle of friends.

Couples and friends dine out on the Vitosha Boulevard, Sofia.

EATING OUT

It is becoming more usual for a foreign acquaintance
to be invited for a night out by his or her Bulgarian
friends. And dining out is what foreigners in Bulgaria
really enjoy—and not just because of the prices. Let's
begin with the great variety of restaurants in the capital
and the other big cities. Apart from restaurants serving
authentic Bulgarian cuisine, all the large international
fast-food chains are available, together with Italian,
Greek, Moroccan, Czech, Russian, Brazilian, Indian,
Japanese, and Chinese restaurants, Irish bars, wine
bars, shisha bars, and everything one would expect in a
multicultural European city. Some restaurants have been
around for many years and have a great reputation, such

Traditional Bulgarian dishes. From top to bottom: cold cucumber soup (*tarator*); baked vegetables in a *sach*; and bean stew (*bob chorba*).

as the Russian Club and the Czech club and restaurant.

Restaurants offering authentic Bulgarian or Balkan cuisine also offer live music and excellent service—quite different from the socialist times of unsmiling waitresses and inflated bills. Customers can join in and learn to dance the *horo*, and perhaps pick up a few lines from their new favorite Bulgarian folk song. You could visit Manastirska Magerniza (the Monastery Refectory) restaurant in Sofia—its menu features recipes collected from monasteries across the country, with dishes such as "drunken rabbit" stewed in wine as well as salads, fish, pork, and the famed monastery bean soup. If you enjoy open-air dining and are in Sofia from late spring to early fall, you can opt for a restaurant like The Bee, located in the heart of the city; it has a huge garden where you can have a romantic dinner "in the forest," with fresh seafood delivered daily.

Bulgarian cuisine shares a lot with its close neighbors. You can try stuffed cabbage or vine leaves as in Greece, Turkey, and Lebanon; cold yogurt cucumber soup as in Cyprus, or its Indian cousin *raita*; barbecued meats; moussaka; vegetable dishes such as *baba ganoush*. An example of typical Bulgarian food is the variety of region-specific stews and dishes in clay pots such as *chomlek*, *kavarma*, and *kapama*. Another trademark of traditional Bulgarian cuisine is *cheverme*—an entire lamb roasted on a skewer. This slow-roast dish originated in the Rhodope region, but it is also served throughout the country.

TIPPING

Bulgaria has adopted the Arabic word *bakshish* for "tip" from Turkish. Tipping is not obligatory in Bulgaria but is a gesture showing satisfaction with the service. In restaurants the customary tip is about 10 percent of the total bill, as waiters make up a part of their salary in tips. If the service and food have been excellent, a higher tip may be given, and is always welcome.

Some taxi drivers simply round up the fare, so to avoid being overcharged it is helpful to have the exact sum of money for the ride. There is absolutely no need to leave *bakshish* if the driver keeps smoking, runs a red light, or asks you not to put your seat belt on because it is too dirty.

Hairdressers are also generally tipped for their service. If you are happy with your new hairdo, the tip is normally between 10 and 20 percent of the charge.

Most public toilets in Bulgaria already charge a compulsory fee. If you come across one where tipping is optional, then be sure to drop 50 *stotinki* (cents of the Bulgarian lev) in the cleaner's box.

NIGHTLIFE

For the young at heart there's clubbing after dinner and Sofia doesn't disappoint. Renowned venues include the likes of Buddha Bar and Chervilo (Lipstick), where guest DJs and themed party nights draw the most fashionable crowds of the capital. Another famous nightclub, Once Upon A Time Biblioteka, is located inside the National Library and is open from Wednesday to Saturday. Many of Bulgaria's favorite DJs started their careers at The Yalta Club, which was the first nightclub to offer electronic music in Bulgaria in the early nineties—it's still going strong today. If you prefer a more laid-back atmosphere, Magnito Piano Bar & Sushi is known for entertaining its visitors with live music and good food, while Piano Bar Jack offers blues and rock at candlelit tables that provide a more intimate atmosphere.

MUSIC, FILM, AND THEATER

Music and dance run in the blood of Balkan peoples. Listen to the sounds and watch the colorful maelstrom at Balkan folk festivals, and you will understand the true meaning of this phrase. Apart from folk music, Bulgarians have made a name for themselves in classical music, too. High culture is much more democratic in Bulgaria than it is in the US. Opera singers such as the soprano Ghena Dimitrova, proclaimed queen of Verdi voices and the first foreigner to be awarded the Giacomo Puccini Prize, was also the first foreign singer to receive an invitation to open a "triple" of the season at La Scala. The great Herbert von Karajan, on hearing her for the first time, exclaimed: "I have lived to hear a voice that only gods deserve!" Opera titan Boris Christoff, one of the greatest basses of the twentieth century, noted for his stage charisma and dramatic temperament, was a praiseworthy successor to the splendid tradition of Slavonic basses such as Feodor Chaliapin and Fyodor Stravinsky. Another Bulgarian, Raina Kabaivanska, one of the leading lyrico-spinto sopranos of her generation, participated in the only opera directed by Maria Callas, *The Sicilian Vespers*, in Turin in 1973. A versatile singer, she is also a talented actress who has performed in several opera movies, including *Tosca*, with Placido Domingo, in 1976.

Although not as famous as the opera singers, Bulgarian pop and rock groups have composed the favorite songs of generations of Bulgarians, and in 1997, Bulgarian pop diva Lilly Ivanova was nominated one of the most famous women of the twentieth century by the International Association of Women.

The first Bulgarian film was the silent comedy *The Bulgarian is Gallant* by Vassil Gendov, which was screened in January 1915 in Sofia. A century of Bulgarian cinema spans the country's turbulent history, and though not as famous as other European cinemas of

The Ivan Vazov National Theater in Sofia.

the twentieth century, it boasts highly respected directors such as Rangel Valchanov, a member of the European Film Academy, whose movie *Where Are You Going?* was shown at the Cannes Film Festival in 1986. A number of Hollywood blockbusters were shot at Nu Boyana film studios in Sofia, including *The Black Dahlia* (2006), *Conan* (2010), *The Expendables 2* (2011), *Olympus Has Fallen* (2012), and *300: Rise of an Empire* (2012), and the studio serviced more than 10 international productions in 2021 alone.

Bulgarian theater has a long history and strong traditions, and there are many vibrant theater scenes

throughout the country. Bulgaria's flagship national theater is a glorious neoclassical venue with 750 seats. Sofia alone has a dozen theaters, including the Satirical, the Army, 199, Sofia, and Tears and Laughter. Bulgarian plays and directors have taken part in Off-Off-Broadway shows since 2001. Unfortunately for those who don't speak the language, the majority of plays and shows are performed in Bulgarian. A night at The National Opera and Ballet, however, should not be missed.

The Roman Amphitheater in Plovdiv, Europe's 2019 Capital of Culture, hosts opera, classical music,

Aerial view of the Roman amphitheater in Plovdiv.

musicals, and theater performances, as well as concerts by the likes of Deep Purple, Sting, Shaggy, Sabaton, and others. See their program at www.oldplovdiv.bg.

FESTIVALS

Bulgaria's cultural scene is a kaleidoscope of events for young and old, amateurs and professionals alike with sixteen regional and international film festivals, over fifty national and international music festivals—

classical, choir, jazz, and ballet—and fifteen classical and puppet theater festivals. All these events are organized by the Bulgarian Ministry of Culture on an annual basis. Here are some of the festivals that should not be missed if you are in the country at the right time.

The Surva International Festival of Masquerade Games takes place every January in the town of Pernik, not far from Sofia. The largest and arguably most impressive of its kind, this festival is dedicated to an ancient pagan ritual, Kukeri, when it was believed that masks and costumes had the power to protect their wearers against evil—the more terrifying the masks, the better. Kukeri festivals are popular throughout Bulgaria.

February is the month to celebrate St. Trifon Zarezan, the patron saint of winemaking. Very early in the morning of February 14, everybody goes to the vineyards. Each vineyard owner digs around his largest vine, pours red wine three times on the roots, and then "feeds" it with special ritual bread, which is afterwards broken and distributed to those present. He cuts three sticks, forms them into a wreath, ties it with a red thread, crosses himself three times, and blesses the vineyard. Then everybody sits down and feasts next to the vines. The producer of the largest quantity of wine throughout the year is proclaimed King of Wine and is blessed by the previous year's king. Then, accompanied by songs and dancing, the king is driven home in an open carriage so that he does not touch the ground, as he is the messenger of God; everyone then crowds into his house, where the festivities continue all night long. As February 14 is also St. Valentine's Day, modern Bulgarians usually like to celebrate both wine and love on the same day, and maybe it's not hard to see why!

Bulgaria produces approximately 70 percent of the world's rose oil, and in June the annual Rose Festival in Kazanlak, in the heart of Bulgarian rose country, celebrates all things related to roses, including the rose oil used in the space industry as greasing because of its resistance to temperature changes. There are three major events: the early morning harvesting ritual in the rose fields, the Rose Queen pageant, and the parade in her honor along the main street of each village. The Rose Festival and the fame of the Bulgarian *damascena* rose attract visitors from all parts of the world, particularly from Japan.

The final unique celebration with the "Only in Bulgaria" label is the July Morning festival on July 1, in the tradition of the great Woodstock festivals of the hippie years. Its name comes from Uriah Heep's hit "July Morning," and it started quite spontaneously in 1980. A day or two before the event people of all ages hitchhike or otherwise travel to the Black Sea to meet the sun on the beach, dedicating the previous evening and the whole night to their favorite music, drinks, and friends. In 2012, more than 12,000 people met the sunrise at Kamen Bryag (Stony Shore), where the song was performed by former Uriah Heep singer John Lawton, who later moved to Bulgaria. In 2022, the festival returned. The date of the July Morning festival could also be related to sun worship and the midsummer-night rites popular throughout Bulgarian lands since time immemorial. Everyone is welcome— no reservation necessary!

For those who would like to sample Bulgaria's pop music, some of the best known artists include Krisko, Galin, Papy Hans, SkandaU, Azis, Divna, Poly Genova, Alex Raeva, Dessy Dobreva, and Hilda Kazasyan.

SPORTS

"God is Bulgarian!" cried the sports commentator Nikolay Kolev "Michmana" ("Midshipman") after Emil Kostadinov's goal eliminated France in the 1994 qualifications for the World Cup.

Under socialism sports were an especially strong focus of attention for the authorities. Ever since the world-renowned, mythically invincible wrestler and catch fighter Dan Kolov, "one true giant in strength and spirit," refused American citizenship, saying, "I am strong because I am Bulgarian," many young and talented Bulgarians have made a name in the world arena, setting standards in sports such as weightlifting, rhythmic gymnastics, sports gymnastics, volleyball, athletics, martial arts, boxing, wrestling, shooting, and many others. Today the country still takes pride in its sporting heroes, but people are mostly fans and spectators.

Grigor Dimitrov at the French Open.

Soccer, or football, can justly claim the title of "favorite national sport," and players Christo Stoichkov and Dimitar Berbatov are a few of the most prominent footballers among a multitude of Bulgarians who have played for teams like Tottenham, Manchester United, Manchester City, Barcelona, Real Madrid, Juventus, Bayern, and many more. In 2013, Berbatov became the first Bulgarian footballer to have played 200 games in the English Championships. He played 305 games and scored 122 goals during his time in England.

Tennis player Grigor Dimitrov became the world number three in singles in 2017.

At the Tokyo Olympics in 2021, Bulgarian women won three gold medals in karate (Ivet Goranova), boxing (Stoyka Krasteva), and overall rhythmic gymnastics (a team effort). Athlete and renowned high

Team Bulgaria at the Gymnastics World Championships in Baku, 2019.

jumper Stefka Kostadinova won the Olympic silver in
Seoul in 1988, gold in Atlanta in 1996, and picked up
a further seven gold medals in world championships.
In 1987, she set a world high jump record of 6 feet
10 inches (2.09 meters), which is still unbroken.

MUST-SEE DESTINATIONS IN AND
AROUND SOFIA

With its long and complex history, natural beauty,
and original art, Bulgaria has something for everyone.
The golden sands of the Bulgarian Riviera will attract
beachgoers; the vast, thickly forested expanses of the
Rhodopes, Rila, and Pirin, with their snow-capped peaks
and emerald-green lakes, will entice trekkers and lovers

Rila Monastery, the largest Orthodox monastery in Bulgaria.

of majestic summits; the traditional music and dances will make your blood run faster; and the warmth and cordiality of the Bulgarians will conquer your heart and bring you back over and over again. However, if you are short of time, there are a few places you really ought to see.

Rila Monastery is a drive of an hour and a half from Sofia, nestled in a valley at the foot of Rila Mountain. Founded in the tenth century CE, it is a great example of Bulgarian national revival architecture. The most impressive frescoes are those showing sinners suffering in an apocalyptic image of Hell.

The Boyana Church is a thirteenth-century medieval church covered in frescoes that predate the European Renaissance by almost a century. It's a UNESCO World Heritage site, located in the suburb of Boyana, Sofia.

The Alexander Nevski Cathedral and its gilt domes are Sofia's most distinctive landmark. An imposing structure in the city center, the cathedral was built to commemorate Russia's role in the liberation of Bulgaria, and named after the Russian medieval military commander and royal prince.

The National Archeology Museum is a converted mosque, offering an impressive collection of ancient and medieval artifacts and treasures.

The National Palace of Culture is a modern congress and concert center whose main hall has excellent acoustics and seats 3,800.

The National Palace of Culture in Sofia.

CHAPTER SEVEN

TRAVEL, HEALTH, & SAFETY

Traveling to and around Bulgaria is generally easy; the country is well connected to the rest of the world, and its infrastructure is being upgraded thanks to EU operational programs. The three major infrastructure projects—the Struma highway connecting Sofia and the Greek border, the Hemus highway connecting Sofia and the city of Varna on the Black Sea coast, and the Black Sea highway, which will connect the coastal cities of Varna and Burgas—are still under construction. One can fly between Sofia and the Black Sea coast cities of Varna and Burgas. Plovdiv has a small international airport but at the time of writing, there are no flights to other Bulgarian cities, bar a few international Ryanair flights a week to Ireland, England, and Germany.

ARRIVAL

Visitors can enter Bulgaria by air, road, rail, or water. Despite its small size, the country has four international airports—Sofia, Varna, Burgas, and Plovdiv—that are well connected with the rest of Europe but that do not currently offer direct flights to North America. To check whether or not you need a visa, visit the Web site of the Bulgarian Ministry of Foreign Affairs (www.mfa.bg), which provides detailed travel information.

Sofia Airport is not a very busy place, so passengers can usually breeze through in a matter of half an hour, including passport control, luggage collection, and customs checks. On leaving the airport it's best to book a taxi with OK SuperTrans who have a counter in the arrivals area. The numerous unsolicited offers you will get should be refused as most taxi drivers will try to rip you off, especially if it's your first visit to the country. For those traveling light, the Sofia subway offers the most efficient and quickest way to get to the city center. There are also regular city buses to and from the airport but be sure to check the timetable. A word of advice: Sofia airport has no luggage room so if you have a long layover and want to see the city, you can leave your luggage in a public locker in the city center, such as those offered by Gifted Sofia (www.giftedsofia.com/en/public-lockers-in-sofia).

Two Black Sea ports and a couple of Danube ports welcome the traveler who arrives by ship. Up until the end of 2009 the Orient Express, immortalized by Agatha Christie in *Murder on the Orient Express*, took its passengers across Europe via Bulgaria to Istanbul, the city straddling Europe and Asia. Today, the country is a part of the pan-European rail network and has direct links to Austria, Hungary, Serbia, and Turkey, as well as Romania, Russia, and Belarus (via the seasonal Black Sea train). The train journey from Sofia to Istanbul takes about eleven and a half hours.

International bus lines such as Eurolines and Flixbus connect all major Bulgarian cities with almost every European capital or larger metropolis. Journeys start and end at the central bus stations (*tzentralna avtogara*) in these cities. Those driving into Bulgaria should be aware of customs regulations and the necessary documentation, which will depend on their citizenship. To drive on Bulgarian roads, you will need a vignette (a sticker showing you've paid). You can buy this at ports, border points, post offices, and large gas stations throughout the country. Stickers can also be bought online at www.vinetki.bg.

All road signs are in Cyrillic script, but some street names and important landmarks are written in English as well. Help yourself get around by using navigation apps such as Google Maps or Waze on your smartphone. For more travel-related apps, see page 196.

MONEY MATTERS

The Bulgarian financial system went through turbulent times in the early 1990s. To stabilize it, a Currency Board was introduced in Bulgaria in July 1997, pegging the local currency—the lev—to major world currencies. This led to improved confidence in the lev, predictable exchange rates, and manageable inflation. After the introduction of the Currency Board, all constraints on trading with foreign currency in the country were removed. Local banks can sell hard currency to private and legal entities without any limitations.

Card payments are now widely accepted, but outside large cities cash still dominates. There is a large network of ATMs that accept standard international credit and debit cards; just make sure you let your bank know you're going abroad so they don't block access to your account. It's best to withdraw reasonable amounts at a time and not to carry a lot of cash at any time.

You may not be able to buy leva from banks and foreign exchange offices in your home country before you leave for Bulgaria, so it's advisable to bring euros that you can change in banks, larger hotels, or exchange bureaux once you've arrived. It's better not to use the exchange bureau at the airport, where the rates are unfavorable. Check the rate of exchange before making a transaction. In 2014, the Bulgarian currency was pegged to the euro: one euro is equal to roughly 1.955 BGN leva.

A tram in downtown Sofia.

GETTING AROUND SOFIA

The best way to get around central Sofia is on foot, but if you are in a hurry use the city's public transportation system or take a taxi. There is a modern metro and a large network of buses, streetcars (trams), and trolleybuses (a cross between a tram and a bus). Buses, streetcars, and the metro run from 5:00 a.m. until midnight, and there are currently four bus routes that run from midnight to 4:00 a.m. See www.sofiatraffic.bg/en for timetables.

The metro in Sofia.

Contactless card payment is now available on all buses, trams, and trolleybuses. At the time of writing, single-trip tickets or a variety of travel cards can still be purchased at the station or from the driver, though these are more expensive and are being phased out in favor of electronic tickets. Metro e-cards are validated at the entrance of metro stations or by touching the card to a pad on buses and trams.

Buses and streetcars can be overcrowded and hot in summer, so your best bet may be a taxi, which is cheap by Western standards. Most taxis are metered, and the yellow cabs are reliable. Tips are not expected, but rounding up the fare is. If you are hailing a taxi on the street, it's advisable to check the fare with the driver before getting into the car.

Internationally popular ride-hailing apps such as Uber and Lyft do not currently operate in Bulgaria. The best local ride-hailing app is TaxiMe; it works with licensed drivers and generally well-maintained cars. Tariffs are standardised and card payments are accepted for payment via the app.

Lime, Bird, and local provider Hobo offer free-floating electric scooters for rent in Sofia. By law, users can't ride on sidewalks and those under the age of 18 are required to wear a helmet. Visitors wishing to go sightseeing can rent an electric bicycle. See www.rentebike.bg for reservations.

TRAVEL OUTSIDE SOFIA

To travel outside the capital, you can choose from a rented car, an intercity bus, a train, a taxi, or, if time is of the essence, a short domestic flight. The national carrier Air Bulgaria offers regular flights between the capital and Varna or Burgas. Train and airplane tickets can be bought online, at the railway or bus station, or from travel offices. Taxis will charge double fare to go to another city. It is possible to share a taxi for long-distance journeys, and taxi drivers will often solicit passengers in front of railway stations.

Train travel is relatively inexpensive and offers passengers beautiful views.

Ridesharing has become more popular in Bulgaria in recent years as a low cost and ecofriendly means of intercity travel. The Tripinfy and 15toGo apps are the most popular apps used locally. Both apps match users with drivers and other riders going the same way.

Buses and Trains

Before the advent of smartphones, fellow travelers on buses and trains used to while away the hours on board by telling stories, discussing politics, playing cards, and sharing food and the occasional beer. Foreigners were granted special attention—or not, because of the language barrier. Nowadays you'll find that most passengers prefer to stare at their phones or laptops, or spend the time talking on the phone. Still, traveling by bus or train is still a relatively inexpensive way to travel the country and offers passengers beautiful scenery.

There are numerous private bus companies operating in Bulgaria, and buses leave several times a day to most destinations. Sofia Central Bus Station has domestic routes to practically everywhere in Bulgaria. There are many ticket counters for all the different operators, and destinations are clearly listed. Tickets are purchased before boarding.

There is an information desk where English will be spoken; otherwise, drivers very rarely speak any language other than Bulgarian, and place names are generally written in Cyrillic. An English-speaking passenger will usually be happy to help.

It is advisable to book in advance during the summer, as vehicles can often be full. Long-distance coaches are air-conditioned, and subtitled English-language movies are shown on monitors during the trip. A bus trip from Sofia to Burgas takes approximately seven hours.

Long-distance trains are also a great way of seeing the country, although they can be quite slow, which is perfect if you're not in a rush as you can sit back and enjoy the scenery. Trainlines connect Sofia, Plovdiv, Burgas, and Varna. Tickets can be purchased at railway stations or in advance at www.bgrazpisanie.com, where train schedules can also be found.

Driving

For those who would rather rent a car and be masters of their own time, a few things are worth remembering. Apart from highway road signs, all other signs are in Cyrillic—something that is usually very confusing for visiting drivers.

Night driving is risky: many roads are in poor condition and road works are often unlit or unmarked. Driving discipline is generally low, and Westerners may find Bulgarian drivers aggressive.

Sticking to the speed limit is essential as it is monitored closely, and fines are levied on the spot. (These can be paid online.)

While there has been considerable progress in eradicating corruption within the police force, old habits die hard, and there are many arbitrary radar speed traps around the country.

Local drivers are well aware of the ingenious ways in which traffic police find concealed spots to catch violators, and they often flash their headlights at oncoming vehicles to warn them of the "trap" ahead.

The traffic police in Bulgaria are generally friendly and polite, and are instructed to identify themselves by name. If you have committed an offense, remain calm, as arguing with an officer will only make matters worse for you—the fine may go up! If you are caught speeding, don't attempt to bribe the traffic police, even if it seems the easier option, as you may find it will backfire.

In a nutshell, if possible, drive around with a Bulgarian friend who knows the roads and how things work, and avoid venturing forth on your own, lest you lose your way, or your sanity.

SOME RULES OF THE ROAD

- Speed limits for cars are 30 mph (50 kmph) inside the city limits, 55 mph (90 kmph) outside cities, and 75 mph (120 kmph) on highways, unless otherwise indicated.
- Driving with dipped-beam headlights or headlights fully on throughout the year, even during the daytime, is compulsory.
- It is compulsory to carry a fire extinguisher, a first-aid kit, a warning triangle, and a reflective jacket. Winter tires are compulsory for vehicles registered in Bulgaria.
- The legal blood-alcohol limit is .05 percent.
- In case of an accident, call 112 or fill out the accident damage form that all drivers are supposed to carry in order to settle insurance claims for minor damage. If you have rented a car, check with your car rental company for arrangements in the event of a breakdown.

HEALTH CARE

Bulgaria has a two-tier health care system: a combination of compulsory health insurance and private medical practice. All residents are entitled to a certain level of insurance coverage with the option to receive supplementary private health care upon covering the extra cost involved. Residents are also entitled to a European Health Insurance Card.

Facilities in most Bulgarian hospitals are basic compared to other EU countries, though the situation has improved in recent years. Bulgarian doctors receive a high level of education and training in four medical universities around the country. In the past, these institutions of higher education attracted a great number of foreign students from Greece, Turkey, and Middle Eastern and African countries. Standards of medical care are acceptable, although specialized equipment and treatment may not be available in provincial medical centers. Hospital staff rarely speak English, especially in the smaller towns. Private clinics and hospitals are generally well equipped and relatively inexpensive, and medical staff working there do generally speak English. Some private hospitals may not accept non-EU health insurance, so it's best to check this with the hospital administration.

If you need emergency medical assistance during your trip, dial 112 and ask for an ambulance. This number can be dialed to reach emergency services—medical, fire, and police—from anywhere in Europe, from any telephone (landline, pay phone, or cell phone). Calls are free. If you are referred to a medical facility for treatment you should contact your insurance/medical assistance company immediately.

NATIONAL EMERGENCY NUMBERS

Ambulance 150

Fire and rescue 160

Police 166

BULSAR (Black Sea search and rescue) 088 161

Car breakdown (in Sofia) 1286

Car breakdown (outside Sofia) 146

On-duty pharmacy 178

If the operator does not speak the language of the caller, he or she selects the caller's language, and the system automatically redirects the call to a speaker of this language.

SAFETY

Serious crime in Bulgaria is rare, and tourists and visitors who use caution and common sense are seldom affected. Organized criminal groups are active, however, within the usual shady trades of running prostitution rings, nightclubs, and casinos. Prostitution is not illegal, but the girls and their pimps are often involved in pickpocketing, mugging, and assaults on foreign clients. Generally Bulgarian women feel safe on the streets, but, as anywhere in the world, all women should take sensible precautions.

Overcharging can happen in bars, nightclubs, and strip clubs, followed by threats when a victim refuses to pay an exorbitant bill.

A trick used by thieves is the deliberate puncturing of car tires, used to distract both driver and passengers, so that the criminals have sufficient time to steal personal belongings and documents from the vehicle. Again, vigilance and common sense are needed at all times, as you would expect when visiting an unfamiliar place where you do not speak the language and are unaware of the local tricks of malevolent individuals bent on robbing you.

Another danger comes from animals. The number of stray dogs roaming the city streets has been steadily decreasing; yet strays are dangerous, especially when they are in a pack. If a dog does bite you, seek help immediately, as rabies is present, though rare, in Bulgaria.

POLICE

It was not prestigious to be a police officer in Bulgaria in the past: policemen were notorious for their lack of intelligence and were the butt of many jokes. Back then they were called "the people's militia," and corruption was rampant. People who were well connected could buy their drivers' licences, bribe their way out of fines, and even avoid jail time for serious offences, thus feeling untouchable and above the law. The rest feared the militia for their violence and brutal attitude to arrested suspects. Things haven't changed much: in summer 2020, police beat participants of the anti-government rallies. While their actions were caught on camera, the Ministry of the Interior refused to show the recordings and even claimed they did not exist. Generally, Bulgarians do not trust the police, and victims often do not report crimes to the police, which risks creating an increase in conventional crime.

Since the early 1990s police applicants have had to pass psychological tests to be accepted into the force; many seek this type of employment because of the stability and newly acquired respectability of the job. The Bulgarian police force is still overwhelmingly male-dominated—very few women apply.

To contact the police, dial 166. The official Web site of the Bulgarian Ministry of the Interior is www.mvr.bg.

CHAPTER EIGHT

BUSINESS BRIEFING

WORK CULTURE

Bulgarian business structure is highly hierarchical: the head office or senior management makes all decisions. This is a reflection of the way Bulgarian society operates—it is very "top–down." The management style is autocratic, with a strict dividing line between bosses and employees. Delegation of authority is a skill that older Bulgarian managers can sometimes lack; younger, Western-educated managers are better at this.

Junior employees readily become friends with each other, sharing their personal joys and problems, but they keep these private issues outside the workplace. Their managers, however, will rarely be in this social group; they could quickly lose face and become the object of rumors if they were to socialize in this way.

SETTING UP A MEETING

Scheduling a business appointment in Bulgaria is done in much the same way as in any other European country. Allow sufficient response time, and avoid official holidays and the summer months. Business appointments are normally planned two to three weeks in advance, preferably by email or by telephone during working hours—typically 9:00 a.m. to 6:00 p.m., Monday to Friday.

It's a good idea to use an intermediary who knows the decision maker personally, if you can. This could significantly reduce your waiting time. Otherwise, contact will be through the executive's personal assistant, and a meeting would probably be scheduled some time ahead, taking its turn according to the diary. An unannounced visit in person would not be welcome, and it's highly unlikely that a meeting would follow then and there.

The introductory meeting is dedicated to personal relations and trust building; it's not a time for presentations or decision-making. Bulgarian businesspeople can be very flexible, and while they may follow the schedule and preferences of their foreign partners, they do not appreciate being rushed; such an approach may make them suspicious, unless they have already established relations of trust with the company or person involved.

GREETINGS AND FIRST IMPRESSIONS

There's a saying in Bulgaria that, "You are received depending on your looks, and seen off according to your brains." Bulgarians treat business meetings formally and show respect by adhering to formal protocols and a conservative dress code.

Appearance is very important for your first impression on a Bulgarian. Good, fashionable, brand-name clothes, spotless, shiny shoes, clean, neat nails, groomed hair, and appropriate accessories will all make the right impression—the positive snap judgment to which Canadian author Malcolm Gladwell refers in his book *Blink: The Power of Thinking Without Thinking*.

A firm handshake, eye contact, and a suitable greeting for the time of day is the norm. It is preferable to address and refer to people by their titles (if you are familiar with them), or to use Mr. (*Gospodin*) or Mrs. (*Gospozha*) in front of the surname. For example, veterinarians or medical doctors are always addressed as "doctor," while Ph.D. holders go by their academic title—professor or docent (associate professor in some European systems of higher education). Only friends and family members would address each other by their first names and give each other a hug or kiss in public. Foreigners should always allow their Bulgarian counterparts to take the lead when their relations become more informal.

Business cards are always exchanged at initial meetings, and having enough cards with you will make a positive impression. It is important not to underestimate the directness of Bulgarians; even though they are more reserved in business situations, they are very clear and explicit. They also have a great sense of humor, which may be used to break the ice.

Leave Enough Time

Note that you should be prepared for a long business meeting. Meetings commonly last longer than the allocated time, so be sure to leave plenty of time between scheduled meetings to allow for this.

Bulgarians will not perceive you as less important if you have nobody with you to take notes or help you with your bags. Your status is judged by your ability to make decisions by yourself. If you arrive with a group, make sure your counterparts know who is who. As hosts, Bulgarian business partners will treat everybody with respect, no matter what their status is, but when it comes to negotiations, they will speak to the person with the highest status.

PRESENTATIONS

Bulgarian businesspeople value their time, so no matter how well constructed and visually impressive it may be, a PowerPoint presentation will be considered a waste of time if it's seen as too long. Your Bulgarian partners would probably rather be offered relevant materials before the meeting so that they can read them and come prepared for discussions. A lively, fact-rich, and entertaining presentation to go with the discussion can be a good idea, though. Your audience will probably sit and watch it silently, but don't be put off if people start whispering to each other during the presentation— this may be a sign of their interest in the subject. Their questions will follow at its end; interrupting a presentation is not considered polite.

NEGOTATIONS

Bulgarian businesspeople are risk-averse, and don't like to hurry over important decisions. They follow the principle "one should measure three times before making the first cut," which makes them less deadline-oriented compared to their Western partners. As we've already seen, another typical attitude is expressed by the saying, "Work is not a rabbit; it won't run away."

The Bulgarian negotiating style is civil and flexible. Business negotiations are usually held with the general executive manager or a high-level executive: they might be accompanied by a negotiating group, but this is more to match the visiting delegation than to discuss and decide collectively. In this case, the manager will listen to his team's suggestions, but in the end, they will make the final decision.

Bulgarians are likely to get straight to the point and discuss the most pressing issues of the business right away. If presented with unanticipated demands, they may ask for additional time, adjourning the negotiating process. If you demand a prompt answer, the reply will most probably be negative, or unsatisfying. The decision-making process is a one-person deal most of the time: the general manager negotiates the deal and can make on-the-spot decisions or take some time to think things over carefully. However, dealing with Bulgaria calls for awareness of the kind of company the foreign firm is negotiating with. If it is owned by one person and managed by another, it is very likely that the owners will be consulted for important decisions. In the cases of mergers, joint ventures, and substantial investments, the board of directors will be consulted first. Decisions are taken unilaterally by the owner/general manager or by a vote of the board of directors in the case of large companies with complex organizational structures.

Bulgarian firms will usually use the services of professional interpreters, translators, and lawyers when conducting negotiations with foreign companies. It would be wise for you to use a Bulgarian lawyer, too. After an agreement is reached, it is best to go over every single detail, delegate tasks, and clarify deadlines, because there is always a chance of misinterpretation.

When discussions come to an end, your Bulgarian counterparts won't leave the negotiating table right away, but instead will stay for a while to have a cup of coffee or tea with you, telling you about the country and asking how you feel about Bulgaria. They will recommend places to visit, and good restaurants, and may extend an invitation to dinner. This is the time to discuss politics, culture, and daily life in Bulgaria, but it will take time before more personal topics, such as family, friends, or details about one's education, are included in the conversation. This is likely to happen after the negotiations have been completed, or even later, once trust has been gained and work relations have been established.

BUSINESS MEALS

Bulgarians like to mix business with pleasure. Negotiations are likely to be followed by long evenings in a local pub or a folklore restaurant, featuring traditional food, drink, music, and dancing. Negotiations are not just about reaching a mutually beneficial agreement but also about helping foreign business partners to enjoy their stay as much as possible and to get to know Bulgaria. The bill is paid by whoever extends the invitation to dinner or orders a round of drinks. Sharing is uncommon and would be considered unusual.

A business lunch in Sofia takes longer than one in London, Frankfurt, or Los Angeles, but remember that a strong stomach, much patience, and amicable relationships are crucial to success when doing business in Bulgaria.

CONTRACTS AND FULFILLMENT

Bulgarian commercial law is based on Roman law: the terms and conditions that would render a contract void or voidable are exhaustively provided for by the law of the land. This is why it is necessary to employ the services of a lawyer familiar with Bulgarian corporate law when drawing up contracts with Bulgarian business partners. As a matter of practice, international business negotiations involving participants from Bulgaria follow generally established models and are up to international standards.

While mutual trust and good personal relationships are key to doing business successfully in Bulgaria, it can take years of cooperation to develop these and the written contract remains vital. Sometimes Bulgarians accept verbal agreements as contractual obligations, but this is not a widespread practice and is not seen in serious business relationships. If a contract includes penalty clauses for missed deadlines or milestones, Bulgarians will pay close attention to any infringements and take them very seriously.

MANAGING DISAGREEMENT

In the event of disputes, both litigation and arbitration are commonly used in Bulgaria. In the past, civil litigation proceedings were drawn out and inefficient. A new Code of Civil Procedure that came into effect in March 2008 is believed to have made the procedures more efficient.

Generally, foreign investors still tend to consider the Bulgarian civil courts to be falling behind the standards needed for effective dispute resolution. Alternative dispute resolutions (ADR), and particularly arbitration, have gained popularity in Bulgaria, saving time and money, and providing confidentiality and more control to the parties involved. Mediation is explicitly recognized by the law; a mediator facilitates the resolution process but does not impose the resolution.

Foreign managers may sometimes have to manage disagreement within the company they lead. Sources of disagreement in the workplace can vary from personal issues to office politics, to labor-related disputes. It is worth remembering that Bulgarian employees expect their boss to make all the decisions and tell them what to do, yet they will also expect appreciation and respect because losing face is highly undesirable. So another no-no is a condescending attitude to one's employees.

BUSINESS GIFTS

Bulgarian businesspeople visiting a foreign company for the first time will generally bring a gift. Statistics show a 20 percent annual growth of the Bulgarian corporate gift market as companies within the country traditionally give and receive gifts on big national holidays such as Christmas, Easter, and St. George's Day. However, giving business gifts is a delicate matter in a country with a relatively high corruption rate. An original, thoughtful gift is better than an expensive one, which might be interpreted in a number of different ways.

Branded office materials, such as promotional notepads, pens, mouse pads, corporate calendars, organizers, USBs, clocks, and ashtrays, are among the most conventional gifts. Other traditional gifts are a bottle of fine wine, a wine rack with accessories, luxury chocolates, or gift baskets of pastries or dried fruit.

Gifts should be appropriate to the recipient's social status and highly respected clients should receive more attention and a more personal present. For company employees' personal occasions, gifts such as vouchers, tours, or flowers are often given.

In Bulgaria gifts are usually opened right away, so that the recipient can express his or her pleased surprise and gratitude.

Bribery and Corruption

The Bulgarian economy offers a number of advantages and disadvantages to people considering establishing a business in the country. One of the weaknesses is the still unresolved problem of bribery and corruption in the public sector, as highlighted by Transparency International's Perceived Corruption Index. On this scale, 0 is highly corrupt and 100 is clean. In 2021, Bulgaria scored 42, which was slightly better than neighboring Albania (35) and Serbia (38).

Following major recommendations by the European Commission, such as increased efficiency through the adoption of active measures by public institutions and increased effectiveness of the legislative framework, petty corruption is becoming less common, and entrepreneurs and companies have stopped paying "taxes" to government officials for undisclosed services.

Bulgaria is in fourth place in the EU with respect to corruption at a personal level, and many Bulgarians who deal with doctors, police officers, or other institutions offer money, a gift, or a favor in order to receive a faster and better service. Such behavior is considered the norm rather than the exception, and has been deeply rooted in the Bulgarian psyche since Ottoman times. A word of advice: if in doubt, ask a trusted local acquaintance to decipher the signs you have noticed and get his or her opinion on how to react.

WOMEN IN BUSINESS

Bulgarian society used to be patriarchal. Men were the breadwinners, and women were in charge of the housework. Communist ideology changed all this: it empowered women by making them socially equal to men and encouraging them to take on typically male jobs in construction, metallurgy, and engineering. Women with "male" professions had a high social status, and received praise, respect, and material rewards. Yet men are still considered "the family head," an attitude that extends into business relations even today—as women are paid less and are promoted less often. Women constantly have to prove themselves, and it is not easy for them to gain respect as professionals. Companies still prefer to hire under-educated and inexperienced men rather than skilled and knowledgeable women, as eventual pregnancy and motherhood might cost them a lot. This might be explained by the fact that Bulgaria provides one of the the longest paid maternity leaves in Europe—410 days— and mothers who prefer to raise their children after this period continue to receive maternity pay until the child turns two.

SOME CULTURAL BLUNDERS

Avoid Statements Like These

"You use the Russian alphabet, don't you?"
"Your language is just like Macedonian."
"Your alphabet was created by the Greeks, wasn't it?"

Avoid

Too much enthusiasm, gesturing, and smiling. This is perceived as fake behavior and will make people suspicious of your intentions.

Avoid These Topics with New Acquaintances

Minorities including the Roma, legal or illegal immigrants, and politics. Human rights, xenophobia, racism, and homophobia in Bulgaria.

CHAPTER NINE

COMMUNICATING

THE LANGUAGE

Bulgarian, an Indo-European language and a member of the southern branch of the Slavonic family of languages, is the first Slavic language of which there is written evidence. The first reference to it as "Bulgarian" appeared in the Greek hagiography of Saint Clement of Ohrid by Theophylact of Ohrid in the late eleventh century.

Immediately after the Second World War, all Bulgarian linguists and most of their foreign colleagues considered the languages spoken in Macedonia and parts of northern Greece to be dialects of Bulgarian. The idea of a federative republic of Southern Slavs, dreamed up by the new Communist governments of Bulgaria and Yugoslavia, led to a policy that attempted to turn Macedonia into the missing link.

In 1945 Macedonian was codified as a separate language, which Bulgaria briefly recognized. Differences emerged with Joseph Tito over the constitution of the new state and the status of the Macedonians, and Stalin was not supportive of the idea, fearing the creation of a strong federation in the Balkans. After the sweeping political changes that started in 1956 (see page 49), Sofia denied the existence of a separate Macedonian language—a position some linguists hold to this very day. However, the current academic consensus outside Bulgaria is that Macedonian is an autonomous language.

In January 2007 the Bulgarian Cyrillic alphabet became the third official alphabet of the European Union. Based on the 2021 Census, 6.95 million people speak Bulgarian as their native language; however, this number does not include speakers outside the country. According to the Bulgarian Academy of Sciences (BAN), approximately 15 million speak Bulgarian worldwide.

EVERYDAY SPEECH

Bulgarian culture is predominantly verbal. Bulgarians are very talkative people who find it hard to be good listeners. Although non-interruption is considered polite, sometimes interrupting is acceptable as a sign of attention and interest. Mediators of meetings, seminars, or training sessions face two problems with a Bulgarian audience: at first nobody will take the floor, but once their initial shyness is overcome, Bulgarians start talking a lot, and it takes a skillful moderator to control the conversation and avoid several groups running their own heated discussions simultaneously.

Quite often, conversations are conducted at high volume and newcomers may even think they're quarrelling. Speaking quietly is not the norm—it is considered a sign that the person is unwilling to communicate and is either insecure or hiding something. So, if you've got something you want to say, don't be shy and speak up!

Good to Know

There are some widely used expressions that can cause misunderstanding:

Da, da / Da be (Yes, yes.) This is the exact match of "Yeah, right"—an expression of disbelief similar to "no way."

Mi sigurno (Well, sure.) An expression of insecurity and doubt, which is commonly misunderstood when taken literally as confirmation.

Shte vidim (We'll see.) This phrase might leave the listener with the impression of uncertainty. In fact, it should be interpreted as a promise, but one without a deadline.

BODY LANGUAGE

Bulgarians gesture a great deal, much like their Mediterranean neighbors. The most notable difference in gestures that you should be aware of is the gestures for "yes" and "no," where in Bulgaria nodding usually means "no," and shaking the head means "yes." Sometimes the "yes" gesture is similar to the "yes" head movement made on the Indian subcontinent. Over the last twenty years, however, many Bulgarians have been educated abroad, or have worked abroad, for long periods of time and so they may nod for "yes" and shake their heads for "no," which can make things then even more confusing. It's best to learn the Bulgarian words for "yes" (*da*) and "no" (*ne*) to make quite sure.

Bulgarians are an emotional lot at heart, and will show their feelings by smiling, grimacing, laughing, scowling, gesturing, and gesticulating. However, the amount of emotion they'll show in any particular situation depends very much on the kind of relationship they have with their interlocutor. They may react emotionally when they are communicating with people they know, but they may seem quite unfriendly and reserved when speaking to strangers.

As far as eye contact is concerned, it is not polite to look for longer than a couple of seconds into a stranger's eyes. However, if people have just met and start talking to each other it is almost obligatory to keep eye contact. In such situations it is a sign of openness, goodwill, and respect. Touching and kissing are allowed only between close friends or relatives. People who are introduced to each other for the first time shake hands. When close male friends meet, they shake hands, too. For men to kiss male friends is considered embarrassing, since they may be perceived as homosexual, and homosexuality is not widely accepted in modern-day Bulgarian society. Men and women kiss each other on the cheek in public only if they are family members or very close friends.

HUMOR

Most foreigners need some time to figure out what makes Bulgarians laugh. Jokes about cultural, ethnic, or other differences may be accepted as funny on the spur of the moment, but they may have a long-term impact on relationships. Bulgarians are quite good at laughing at themselves, yet foreigners may find the Bulgarian sense of humor too direct and insulting at times, since Bulgarians often make politically incorrect jokes.

Anything can be the subject of humor—corrupt politicians, dumb cops, sexist jokes, jokes about minorities like Roma, Jews, and Armenians, or clever and conniving folk characters such as Sly Peter (Hitar Petar) or *Shopi* (people living in parts of Western Bulgaria). Comedy and satirical shows have always been popular, and comedians are the darlings of Bulgarian audiences. Nikolaos Tzitiridis is a famous Bulgarian comedian who has his own TV show. The Comedy Club Sofia mostly hosts local comedians in Bulgarian, but foreign stand-up comedians perform in the club occasionally, including Louis C.K. in 2019.

Have You Heard About . . . ?

The city of Gabrovo is known for its distinctive humor, and many local jokes revolve around the alleged stinginess of its citizens. Here is a typical Gabrovo-style joke: Why don't people from Gabrovo buy refrigerators? Because they can't be sure the light goes off when the door's closed.

Thickheads (*bortsi* or *vratove*) are the Bulgarian mafia's low-level operatives and bodyguards who stereotypically drive luxury cars, have no brains, and can be extremely violent. They are also the butt of many Bulgarian jokes:

A thickhead is zooming along the highway in his BMW when his cell phone rings.
"Hey man, where are you?"
"I'm driving on the highway, why?"
"Be very careful, the radio just announced that some maniac is doing 300 kmph the wrong way on the highway!"

"It's not just one, man, there are dozens of them!"

The name of the *Shopi* ethnic group in Bulgaria is frequently used as a mocking nickname, as a synonym of a simple, wild, conservative man, or as a synonym of a sly, crudely practical man, able to find a way out of any situation.

A woman says to her lover: "Nane, I want you to desire me like Romeo, be jealous like Othello, and make love to me like Casanova!" The man answers: "Peno, I can only bite your ass 'cause I've only read *The Hound of the Baskervilles*."

THE MEDIA

Television

There is one state television broadcaster (Bulgarian National Television), offering three channels: BNT1, BNT2, and BNT World. Privately owned television companies in Bulgaria are bTV (six channels) and NOVA television. TV channels are in fierce competition and offer many homemade serials, shows, and popular foreign sitcoms. Bulgarian cable TV Eurocom is another popular channel offering a variety of highly popular talk shows like "EuroDikoff" and "Honestly."

The Covid-19 pandemic brought about the birth of some extremely popular YouTube and Facebook channels, followed by hundreds of thousands of viewers thirsty for alternative sources of information, different from the official, government-supported and controlled television channels (in 2022, Bulgaria ranked 91st out of 180 in the World Press Freedom Index).

While television is still the main source of "official" information in Bulgaria (followed by newspapers and radio), many people are also informed by information they come across on social media platforms where the hot topics of the day are widely discussed.

Radio

For many years prior to 1990 Bulgarians had been listening to the two channels of the National Radio: Horizon and Hristo Botev. Today a private radio station, Darik, is the third channel with national coverage. The sweeping political changes brought more than four dozen private radio stations with regional coverage, most of them dedicated to a certain musical style, such as jazz, folk, or *chalga* (a mix of folk and pop).

Print and Online Media

There is a long tradition of journalism in Bulgaria, and Bulgarians have always been avid newspaper readers, which explains the abundance of dailies, weeklies, tabloids, and specialized publications on culture, finance, education, health and well-being, to mention a few. With the advent of the Internet many dailies like the *Standart News* (the third-largest Bulgarian newspaper) run bilingual Bulgarian/English editions online. Other online sources of Bulgarian news are Frog News (culture, sports, and tourism), Novinite (www.novinite.com), a major news provider in English, *Media Times Review* (an online magazine for politics, economy, and culture) and the *Sofia Echo*—a weekly English-language newspaper. A more recent addition is the independent news site Sofia Globe (www.sofiaglobe.com), which offers up-to-date English-language updates and analysis on Bulgarian, European, and world news.

INTERNET AND SOCIAL MEDIA

Bulgarians were quick to embrace the Internet and today, the country's Internet speeds are among the top ten fastest in the world, according to the Speedtest Global Index. Visitors to Sofia will find that free Wi-Fi is virtually omnipresent.

Online services in Bulgaria have come a long way in recent years and today all banks and utility suppliers offer their services online. Most government offices also offer online services. All government services can be found at www.e-gov.bg, where an English-language option is available.

According to the latest EU statistics, there

are 4.9 million daily Internet users in Bulgaria, which amounts to approximately 71 percent of the population. Of these, 4.3 million (62 percent) have some form of social media account. The most popular platform used locally is Facebook (by a long way), followed by YouTube and Instagram.

There are several Bulgarian copycat social networks and bookmarking sites, which allow you to stay up to date with what is going on in the country, including upcoming events and breaking news. Svejo.net is used to share Web sites, video content, and pictures. If the content is new and interesting, it immediately becomes "Fresh" (*svejo* in Bulgarian) and is promoted on the home page of the site. The Web site www.lubimi.com ("Favorites") is a social network that is good for publishing articles from various blogs, allowing shared links to be followed by search engines. Some more socially oriented networks, like www.twist.bg, allow users to share links, news, videos, and event listings, and www.idi.bg ("Go") is the Bulgarian version of Booking.com, offering a variety of places for relaxation and vacationing. Vbox7 is the Bulgarian version of YouTube and is well used by both businesses and personal users.

SERVICES

Telephone

Vivacom BTC (Bulgarian Telecommunications Company) is the national provider of telephone services. The company offers a wide variety of packages for home telephone lines and packages are available for local, long distance, and international calls; there are reduced charges for people with disabilities and plans for minimal usage. Many people are forgoing landlines in favor of cell phones.

Bulgaria's cell phone network covers the whole country. Cell phone usage is widespread, and foreigners who bring their own phones to the country are unlikely to face any problems. To save on roaming charges, though, visitors can opt for a pre-paid SIM card from a Bulgarian cell phone operator such as Yettel Bulgaria (www.yettel.bg), A1 (www.a1.bg), or Vivacom (www.vivacom.bg), so that they can make calls to Bulgarian numbers at local prices. All they need is an unlocked phone.

Mail

Postal services in Bulgaria are becoming more efficient, yet the delivery of mail, especially to a newly built Bulgarian home, is still hit and miss, so many expats have a mailbox in the local post office. Properly formatted addresses on envelopes help delivery reliability; the format is usually displayed in post offices, and you should explain it to people who are likely to send you mail. Here's an example of how the information should be listed:

Plovdiv 4002 (City and postal code)
63 Karl Marx Str. (Building no. and street)
Peter Pavlov (Name)

The number of courier companies is also growing. Together with well-established international giants such as DHL, there are local, privately owned courier services such as Europat, Ekont Express, and Speedy.

CONCLUSION

The three emblems of ancient gold treasures, rose oil, and wine symbolize the distinctive culture of this beautiful land. The youngest member of the European Union, Bulgaria has been riding a roller coaster of radical political and economic transformation for over thirty years, developing in many ways while preserving its own particular charm and slow-paced way of life. Although Bulgarians can easily be mistaken for Greeks, Italians, or Spaniards because of their looks and their fondness for the beautiful and fashionable, underneath their modernity and physical similarities runs a profound sense of tradition. It is the survival of this tradition that makes Bulgaria so intriguing and not just another former communist country on its way to democracy and a market economy. Tradition was the Bulgarians' secret weapon, ensuring their cultural survival during the long centuries of foreign domination, and it continues to be their main source of pride and national identity.

The Bulgarians are self-reliant, resourceful, and pragmatic—skills they had to develop to survive foreign rule and dictatorial regimes. The visitor may find them a baffling mix of characteristics at times: flexible and open to outside influences, yet risk-averse and unwilling to become trailblazers; compliant or even servile, yet mistrustful of authority. They may be pessimistic at times, yet they never stop aspiring to a brighter future for their children. They may be a little jealous of the wealth of others, but they work hard all their lives to fulfill their purpose. They may not be rich, but their hearts and homes are always open to friends from near and far. Above all, Bulgarians place their trust in friends and family, and welcome visitors with the traditional offerings of bread and salt, a red rose, and a wooden vessel of sparkling wine. We hope that *Culture Smart! Bulgaria* has helped you to discover one of Europe's best hidden secrets.

FURTHER READING

Charry, Frederick B. *The History of Bulgaria*. Westport, Connecticut: Greenwood, 2011.

Dasgupta, Rana. *Solo*. Boston: Houghton Mifflin Harcourt, 2011.

Daskalov, Roumen. *Debating the Past: Modern Bulgarian History from Stambolov to Zhivkov*. Budapest: Central European University Press, 2011.

Greenwell, Garth. *What Belongs to You*. New York: Picador, 2016.

Groueff, Stephane. *Crown of Thorns: The Reign of King Boris III of Bulgaria 1918–1943*. Aurora, Ontario: Madison Books, 1998.

Kaplan, Robert. *Balkan Ghosts: A Journey through History*. New York: Picador, 2005.

Kassabova, Kapka. *Border: A Journey to the Edge of Europe*. London: Granta Books, 2017.

Kassabova, Kapka. *A Street without a Name: Childhood and other Misadventures in Bulgaria*. New York: Skyhorse Publishing, 2009.

Konstantinov, Aleko. *Bai Ganyo: Incredible Tales of a Modern Bulgarian*. Madison: Wisconsin University Press, 2010.

Kostova, Elizabeth. *The Shadow Land*. New York: Ballantine Books, 2017.

Ovcharov, Dimiter. *Fifteen Treasures from Bulgarian Lands*. Sofia: National Museum of Bulgarian Books and Polygraphy, 2003.

Penkov, Miroslav. *East of the West: A Country in Stories*. New York: Farrar, Straus and Giroux, 2011.

Phoel, Cynthia Morrison. *Cold Snap: Bulgaria Stories*. Dallas, Texas: Southern Methodist University Press, 2010.

Simeon II of Bulgaria. *A Unique Destiny: Memoirs of the Last Tsar of Bulgaria, Prime Minister of a Republic*. Mechanicsburg, Pennsylvania: Stackpole Books, 2021.

Borina publishing house (www.borina.com) offers a variety of illustrated books about Bulgarian culture, history, geography, and the arts.

USEFUL APPS

Communication and Entertainment

Google Translate Translate menus and road signs using the camera function, or get the pronunciation for words and phrases in Bulgarian that you want to say.

Nova Play is an app offering shows from Bulgaria's Nova TV, Kino Nova, Diema и Diema Family.

Voyo is a paid streaming service for watching movies, TV films, sports events, and concerts.

Vbox7 popular Bulgarian portal for video sharing.

Travel and Transportation

Bulgarito Discover Bulgaria's most popular travel destinations. (Android only.)

Moovit Route planning app that includes public transportation schedules in all the major cities.

Sinoptik.bg is the most popular weather forecast app.

TaxiMe Sofia's most popular hail-a-ride app.

Food and Shopping

Glovo Food delivery app operational in Sofia and other large cities.

Grabo.bg is the local variant of Groupon. It offers vouchers for dining out, entertainment, medical and cosmetic services, travel, and sports at discounted prices. Customers can pay in cash, by card, via ePay, or PayPal.

OLX.bg is the Bulgarian eBay. With close to three million ads, it's the largest free portal in the country.

Pazaruvaj is a price-comparison platform for those looking for good deals.

Takeaway.com Food delivery in Bulgaria's major cities.

PICTURE CREDITS

Copyright © 2023 Kuperard

INDEX

Acknowledgments

To my parents who taught me to love my country; to my friends who have always been loyal and trustworthy, and to my family who have always supported me. Thank you!